THE C.A.M.P. COOKBOOK

Borgo Press Books by VICTOR J. BANIS

*The Astral: Till the Day I Die * Avalon: An Historical Novel * The C.A.M.P. Cookbook * The C.A.M.P. Guide to Astrology * Charms, Spells, and Curses for the Millions * Color Him Gay: That Man from C.A.M.P. * The Curse of Bloodstone: A Gothic Novel of Terror * Darkwater: A Gothic Novel of Horror * The Daughters of Nightsong: An Historical Novel (Nightsong Saga #2) * The Devil's Dance: A Novel of Terror * Drag Thing; or, The Strange Tale of Jackle and Hyde * The Earth and All It Holds: An Historical Novel * A Family Affair: A Novel of Horror * Fatal Flowers: A Novel of Horror * Fire on the Moon: A Novel of Terror * The Gay Dogs: That Man from C.A.M.P. * The Gay Haunt * The Glass House: A Novel of Terror * The Glass Painting: A Gothic Tale of Horror * Goodbye, My Lover * The Greek Boy * The Green Rolling Hills: Writings from West Virginia (editor) * Green Willows: A Novel of Horror * Kenny's Back * Life & Other Passing Moments: A Collection of Short Writings * The Lion's Gate: A Novel of Terror * Love's Pawn: A Novel of Romance * Lucifer's Daughter: A Novel of Horror * Moon Garden: A Novel of Terror * Nightsong: An Historical Novel (Nightsong Saga #1) * The Pot Thickens: Recipes from Writers and Editors (editor) * San Antone: An Historical Novel * The Scent of Heather: A Novel of Terror * The Second House: A Novel of Terror * The Second Tijuana Bible Reader (editor) * The Sins of Nightsong: An Historical Novel (Nightsong Saga #3) * Spine Intact, Some Creases: Remembrances of a Paperback Writer * Stranger at the Door: A Novel of Suspense * Sweet Tormented Love: A Novel of Romance * The Sword and the Rose: An Historical Novel * This Splendid Earth: An Historical Novel * The Tijuana Bible Reader (editor) * Twisted Flames * The WATERCRESS File: That Man from C.A.M.P. * A Westward Love: An Historical Romance * White Jade: A Novel of Terror * The Why Not * The Wine of the Heart: A Novel of Romance * The Wolves of Craywood: A Novel of Terror*

THE C.A.M.P. COOKBOOK

WITH THE HELP OF LADY AGATHA & JACKIE HOLMES

VICTOR J. BANIS

THE BORGO PRESS

MMXII

DEDICATION

To "Don Holliday," without whose help this would have been impossible, and to the entire C.A.M.P. staff, whose advice and help have proved invaluable, and to Jackie and Rich, whose constant prodding and encouragement led it its completion.

To those "Three on a Broomstick": Patty, Verna, and Maude, for the loan of the facilities of their test kitchen.

To Sophie, whose constant willingness to test all recipes proved an invaluable aid (although at some times a nuisance).

And especially to my co-conspirator, Lady Agatha.

I am also deeply indebted to my friend, Heather, for all the help she has given me in getting these early works of mine reissued.

And I am grateful as well to Rob Reginald, for all his assistance and support.

To all of these my sincerest thanks.

—Victor J. Banis

Contents

CHAPTER ONE

When the Queen Is in Her Kitchen (Getting Acquainted)

And away we go! Back to that little room. No, not that one—the one just on the other side of that place they call the dining area. The kitchen, of course. Now, I'm sure you know your way around the other rooms, especially the one with the queen-sized you-know-what; but as I'm *prone* to mention from time to time, one of the ways to a man's heart is through his stomach, which means that you'll have to spend some time in the kitchen cooking (and unfortunately washing dishes, etc.).

Let's assume that it's your first very own kitchen, and you don't have a pot to put peas in. So what's our first project? Equipment. Isn't it always?

Now you don't need every little fancy gadget that you can find at the five-and-dime, but there are basics—let's stick to them. A cast-iron skillet works just as well as one that's coated with pastel porcelain, and costs a hell of a lot less. And if you look in one of your local thrift shops, you can probably find a used one at a small fraction of what a new one costs. The fact that it is already black is actually a prestige symbol, too: it doesn't make you look so much like a novice and can actually aid in giving you confidence.

Personally. I take advantage of every opportunity to shop for bargains in the Goodwill and Salvation Army stores—the prices are very lean and most items are in wonderful condition. If one of your sisters should be so crass as to ask where you got that "awful looking casserole," just tell her that it belonged to your dear, departed great-grandmother.

Now, how are we going to equip ourselves (I mean, kitchen-wise)? First of all we'll need:

SAUCE PANS—For your first experiments, two should be enough. I recommend that you have one two-quart pan and one with a one-quart capacity. Later you will want to get a small one-pint pan and perhaps more of the other sizes. Make sure that they have lids, tight-fitting ones. Many foods have to be covered, and although we could, in a pinch, simply set a plate or saucer on top of the pan, it isn't entirely satisfactory.

SPOONS—I would recommend an investment (less in the thrift stores) in a set of four or five wooden spoons for stirring. Later on I would certainly get a ladle and a slotted spoon, but they're not necessary at the start.

FRYING PAN—Get about a ten-inch skillet to start with, and again, one with a lid. If you find you need a larger size later on, you can always get it—but there's no use investing in one of the little tiny ones, except for the sake of convenience.

SPATULA—The broad type used by short-order cooks to turn hamburgers is the best all-round variety. There are others, too, and if your pocketbook allows or your vanity decrees, you may add them to your collection. But for pity's sake, take into consideration the amount of storage space you have. We want to be able to move around in this little room, and find things easily.

KNIVES—At least two to start. One chef's or French knife, which is used primarily for chopping and cutting vegetables, but is easily adaptable to slicing meats as well; and one paring knife, which we'll be using for all sorts of things. Others you might want to add to your collection eventually are a roast knife, a boning knife, a butcher knife, and a slicer. These all make particular jobs a little bit easier, but they are not absolutely essential.

MIXING BOWLS—A set of four nested or individual bowls of four different sizes. Buy them at the thrift shop, but please make sure they're glass or crockery. Plastic and metal bowls do funny things to food at times.

MEASURING CUPS AND SPOONS—The former usually come in a set of four (quarter-cup, third-cup, half-cup, and one cup). The spoons also come in a set of four (quarter-teaspoon, half-teaspoon, one teaspoon, and one tablespoon). If you can get metal ones, you'll find they will hold up better.

COFFEE POT—Any kind. The thrift stores usually have a good variety, take your choice: dripolator, percolator, or vacuum type; but we must have available a way to make REAL coffee.

CAN OPENER—Electric or hand-operated. No, not that way. If you don't have one now, try plunging a good, stiff blade into your can and work it around until you're satisfied (that the hole is big enough).

BOTTLE OPENER—The "church-key" variety is best, most versatile and cheapest.

VEGETABLE BRUSH—The "loop" kind is the easiest to use. Just plunge a long, pliable carrot in the bristle-lined hole and vigorously jam it in and out until the thin skin is worn away.

EGG BEATER—Sadistic cooks (the same ones who crack nuts by hand rather than buying the pre-shelled kind) prefer the manual beaters for frothing up the slimy albumen. You can save for an electric mixer.

Now your kitchen is adequately equipped to prepare dishes fit for a queen.

There is other kitchen equipment that you are going to need, some immediately, like dish towels, sponges, detergent, hot pads, etc. But I'm sure you can take care of those items yourself, with perhaps the counsel of a friendly sister. When you get into the more ambitious recipes in this book, they might call for special items, and you can get them when the times comes. Some of the basics among these that you will want to purchase from time to time, as the pocketbook allows, are:

ROASTING PAN WITH RACK—Get a big enough one, but not too big for your oven.

BAKING SHEET—Not only for cookies, but also as a drip pan for those nights you are (but hopefully never) alone and you simply heat a TV dinner.

COLANDER—A tennis racket might be all right in the movies for draining spaghetti, but it sure plays hell with your tennis game. Try the bowl type with small holes (not too small—you might strain yourself).

SOUP KETTLE WITH LID—At least a six-quart capacity for those gay times when friends drop in unannounced.

CASSEROLES—According to the recipe, you'll probably have more than one eventually.

PIE PLATE—At least one nine-incher. (Mmmm!)

GRATER—There's an excellent plastic one on the market that cleans easily and reduces the danger of cutting your fingers.

SALAD BOWL, FORK, AND SPOON—Wooden, of

course.

ROLLING PIN—This has multiple uses. Use your imagination.

CORKSCREW—Not an essential item at first, and sometimes it's fun to carry a bottle of wine to the door of interesting neighbors in search of this little item. So much more original than asking for a match or borrowing a cup of gin.

STRAINER—A very handy item, and should be about teacup size.

MEAT FORK—The heavy duty, two-tined variety.

RUBBER SCRAPER—For mixing and getting the last drop of creamy sauces out of a thing.

TIMER—In case you're forgetful.

WHISK—In any of several convenient size or sizes— just to make you feel more like Julia Child.

Now on to our basic stocking of the pantry (which has nothing to do with pants). These are simply the necessary staples that you should have in your kitchen at all times so you can whomp up a meal on a moment's notice. I've checked over several suggested lists, and most of them look like they were planned for the siege of Troy. Here we shall list only those items which yours truly likes to have on hand, but unfortunately doesn't always:

Bacon
Baking Powder
Baking Soda
Bouillon cubes—beef, chicken, and vegetable
Bread
Butter (or margarine)
Cheese (cheddar and whatever else your little heart desires)
Cocoa (I prefer the instant variety)
Coffee
Condiments (catsup, prepared mustard, Worcestershire sauce, etc.)
Crackers (saltines and those little cocktail goodies)
Eggs
Fish—tuna, salmon, clams, and other favorite canned varieties.
Flavor extracts—especially vanilla, maybe almond and rum.
Flour—all-purpose is best.
Garlic
Herbs and spices—we'll talk about these in a moment.
Lemon juice
Lettuce
Mayonnaise
Meat—whatever you're planning for the next two or three days, and perhaps a few canned varieties as well. If you have a freezer, you can store a reserve supply there for emergencies.

Milk

Mushrooms—canned

Nuts—slivered, toasted almonds, and any other favorites.

Oil—salad or cooking, and olive if desired.

Olives, green

Potatoes, baking and boiling

Rice—the quick-cooking variety is handiest.

Soups—a variety of dried and canned.

Sugar—white granulated. Other varieties can be purchased as needed, although it might be wise to keep a small amount of dark brown sugar on hand as well.

Syrup—maple, for pancakes.

Tea—in bags is fine.

Vegetables—a variety of both canned, and if you have a freezer, frozen.

Vinegar—red and white wine varieties.

Wines—I like to keep a stock for drinking and cooking. More detail on this in the next chapter.

Now, I promised to let you know the intimate secrets of my spice shelf, so here are the ones that I never want to be without:

Basil

Bay Leaves

Chili Powder

Cinnamon—stick and powdered

Cloves—whole and powdered

Curry Powder

Mace
Marjoram
MSG
Mustard—dry powder
Nutmeg
Oregano
Paprika
Pepper—black
Rosemary
Sage
Salt
Savory
Tarragon
Thyme

Many of the recipes in this book will call for these. Others you will find use for as you gain experience in cooking and acquaintance with the nature of each of the herbs and spices. Additional uses for these are generally listed on the cans or bottles.

* * * * * * *

All set? Let's look now at how we should follow a recipe, how to measure various ingredients, and all sorts of other helpful little hints that will enable us to avoid having our little bailiwicks declared a disaster area.

When you are getting ready to prepare a certain dish, first read the recipe all the way through. If the first reading doesn't give you a clear picture of what is to be done, read it through again with extra care. Make a note of all the ingredients that are necessary, and of all the equipment—and make sure that all are on hand before you start your preparation. If this is your first try at following the recipe, keep your cookbook open for reference. You might even want to do this for at least the first several times you prepare a dish.

I'd like to know just who it was that said that a cook should cook without a book. Musicians, doctors, lawyers, and even writers make constant reference to their libraries, and I think that a cook should have the same prerogative. Of course, there will be items that you will learn well enough through practice that you won't have to make reference to a book, and that's all well and good. But there are others where particular attention to detail is of the utmost importance, and in those cases, I say use the book.

In measuring, we will stick basically to the standard cups and spoons in our collection as specified above. Wherever another happens to be specified, we shall discuss it at that point. In general, when preparing a recipe it is best to measure the dry ingredients first; filling the measure and then leveling off with the straight (pardon the expression) edge of the knife. Flour should be sifted before measuring (but if you don't have a sifter, there are certain varieties on the market known as pre-sifted), and in contrast, brown sugar should be packed down tightly. Other types of dry ingredients fall between these two categories, and should only be slightly shaken to be sure that there are no air bubbles that might throw off the measure.

Liquid ingredients are much simpler. Simply fill the measure to the brim.

Butter, shortening, and other solid fats are most easily measured by what is known as the displacement method. Say your recipe calls for a quarter-cup shortening. In your one-cup measure, put three-fourths cup water, then add butter (or shortening or whatever) until the water reaches the brim. Pour off the water and you're left the right amount of butter.

The following table of equivalents may prove of value to you at times:

3 teaspoons equals 1 tablespoon
2 tablespoons equals 1 ounce
8 ounces equals 1 cup
2 cups equals 1 pint
2 pints equals 1 quart
4 quarts equal 1 gallon

Two other important items in following a recipe are: (1) doneness (it's important to know when a thing is done), which we'll discuss separately for each recipe, and (2) a little item called "to taste." In innumerable cases it is impossible to tell just how much of a particular ingredient to add, and this is especially true in regard to such items as salt, pepper, and some herbs, spices, and condiments. Therefore, you will have to rely on your own taste, adding what you think it necessary, and then tasting to see if the amount if sufficient—be careful, though not to add too much. It's easier to add ingredients than it is to subtract them.

I'm reminded of the time when Paulette and I had just set up housekeeping and were serving a brunch for eight people. She had just beaten the eggs and added the salt. When she took the top off the coarse pepper bottle she forgot that it didn't have a shaker top and as a consequence poured the whole bottle into the gooey mess. Brunch was delayed for about an hour while we strained the icky stuff through a sieve. Brunch was saved, but you can see what a timesaver a little care can be.

I think it's rather safe to assume that the majority of meals that you'll be serving will be dinners, so we'll consider a very basic type menu from which you can build all kinds of tasty fare:

Cocktail (may be omitted)—consists of juice, fruit, shrimp, or other light opener.

Soup and/or Salad—in general, when soup is served the salad is served with the main course.

Main Course or Entrée—meat, fish, or fowl.

Starchy Course—potatoes, rice, or pasta.

Green or Yellow Vegetable—this and the starchy course are generally served with the entrée.

Bread and Butter—also served with the main course, and sometimes appearing as early as the soup or salad course.

Dessert—often omitted when soup and/or salad is served.

Wine (if desired)—more about this in another chapter.

Coffee and Liqueurs—after dinner, although many people prefer to have coffee with dinner.

Plan your menu according to the appetites and tastes of your guests. They are of prime consideration. It is also somewhat embarrassing to put together a lamb curry and find that one guest can't stand lamb and another is allergic to curry—and watch the calendar, too. Some of your friends might abstain from eating meat on Friday.

Plan around your main course, taking into consideration the color and texture of the foods that you plan to serve. A variety of colors makes, generally, for an attractive meal, and is rather simple to plan. The addition of a sauce or garnish such as parsley or watercress tends to spark up the appearance of food. But beware of over-saucing. Beef Stroganoff served with creamed potatoes and asparagus with Hollandaise presents a platter smothered with too much of the same texture. What do I mean by texture? Creamy or chewy, soft or crisp, thick or thin, clear or cloudy—these are textures. Take them into consideration and make sure that your menus do not include too much sameness.

The same principle applies to individual foods. Just imagine a dinner where the soup course was cream of mushroom, the salad included chopped mushrooms, the entrée was steak and mushrooms served with stuffed mushrooms, and dessert was (and there is such a thing) mushroom chocolate cookies. Tired of mushrooms?

Let your conscience and your imagination be your

guide, and you'll seldom go wrong. In leaving this subject, let us touch upon just one more point—don't serve too little, don't serve too much. Both are embarrassing, the first to the host and the second to the guest.

Timing is the next item of consideration. It's very important that all items are ready to serve at the proper times. It does little to enhance your reputation as a cook if the potatoes are done and the roast still has an hour to cook. Many trials and tribulations can be avoided by doing as much preparation as possible in advance. For instance, you can prepare the greens and dressing for your salad and keep them in the fridge, as long as they are separate, hours before you serve them. And many vegetables can be prepared for cooking long in advance—in spite of any ranting and raving and carrying on that I might do later in discussing their proper treatment.

The basic idea behind all this ahead-of-time preparation, is that when you are beginning, you are not thoroughly familiar with the time involved in preparation (recipes only list cooking time). As you start finding your way around the kitchen as well as you do around the bedroom, you'll start sandwiching these preliminary steps between other operations. But at first, not only plan ahead, but do ahead as well.

Start things cooking in reverse order. In other words, start with those that take the longest time, then work up to the quick cookers last. It might be well at first, especially if you're going to be mingling with your guests over drinks, to make a written notation of the time everything should be started—at least at first. Later on it'll become second nature.

* * * * * * *

A small vocabulary is now in order—and I'm going to eliminate a lot of items that other cookbooks have. At the present time you're not going to be interested in the fact that *asperges* is French for asparagus and not a form of slander, or that a Bain Marie is the bottom pan of a chafing dish and not an expression meaning keep Mary out of the bar. I trust you will find it helpful and basic. Basic things are important.

Bake—To cook by dry contained heat, usually in an oven. Applied to meats, it is called roasting.

Baste—To moisten foods during cooking with pan drippings, water, wine, or sauces to prevent drying and/or add flavor.

Beat—To briskly whip or stir with a spoon or rotary beater in order to make a mixture smooth or add air to it.

Blend—To combine ingredients until smooth.

Boil—To cook in boiling liquid (212 degrees F. at sea level).

Braise—To brown in small amount of fat, then add a small amount of liquid and cook slowly on top of stove or in oven, tightly covered.

Bread—To coat with bread crumbs or cracker crumbs (sometimes crushed wheat or corn flakes). Sometimes the item to be breaded is first dipped in a mixture of beaten egg and milk.

Broil—To cook by direct heat, in a broiler, under flame or over coals.

Brown—It's different in the kitchen. To cook in hot fat until brown in color.

Chop—To cut in pieces with scissors or a knife. (If you're going to use scissors, I would recommend that you have a separate pair for kitchen use only.)

Cream—Didn't know cooking could be so C.A.M.P.y, did you? This means to rub...stir...or beat. But with a spoon until a mixture is soft, creamy, and smooth.

Cut—In addition to the obvious meaning of separation into pieces by scissors or knife, it also means the combination of shortening with dry ingredients by means of a pastry blender or two knives. I prefer to discard the utensils and use my lily white hands.

Dice—To cut into small cubes.

Dissolve—To mix a dry substance in a liquid until it passes into solution.

Dredge—To coat with flour or other specified fine substance.

Flake—To break into small pieces (as tuna).

Fold—To combine ingredients by cutting down through mixture with your tool, sliding it across the bottom and bringing it up and over top close to the surface. The tool you use, however, should he a spoon, whisk, or fork.

Fricassée—To braise fowl or rabbit.

Fry—To cook in hot fat, as directed.

Garnish—To decorate foods with small pieces of

colorful ones, such as parsley, pimentos, or egg slices.

Glaze—To coat with a thin sugar syrup.

Grate—To separate food in various sizes of bits or shreds by rubbing on a grater.

Knead—To work and press dough to smoothness with the palms of the hands.

Marinate—To allow a food to stand in a liquid (usually flavored) to soften or add flavor.

Melt—To heat a substance until it liquefies.

Mince—And I don't mean down Main Street. You can camp in your kitchen, but this means to chop into tiny pieces.

Mix—To stir, and thus combine ingredients.

Pan-broil—To cook uncovered in a hot skillet. Pour off fat as it accumulates.

Parboil—To cook partially, by boiling.

Pare—To cut away the outer covering or skin.

Peel—To remove outer covering by stripping, as a banana.

Pit—To remove the seeds from fruits. Not yours, honey.

Poach—To cook in hot liquid, taking care that foods hold their shape.

Roast—See bake.

Sauté—To cook in small amount of hot fat. Whether you're pan-frying or sautéing depends on the food you're cooking.

Scald—To bring a liquid to a temperature just below boiling.

Score—No, this doesn't mean to make out. It means to cut narrow gashes in the outer covering of food.

Sear—To brown quickly with intense heat. Before you hop on the stove, better refer back to the kitchen definition of brown.

Shred—To cut or tear into ribbon-like pieces.

Sift—To pass dry ingredients through a sieve.

Simmer—To cook slowly over low heat, usually about 185 degrees.

Steam—A delicious way to prepare vegetables, but since we're not going to do it at first, I won't discuss it further.

Steep—To extract color or flavor from a substance by letting it stand in water just below the boiling point.

Stew—To simmer slowly in a small amount of liquid for a long time.

Stir—To mix ingredients until blended with a circular motion of a fork or spoon.

Toast—To brown by direct heat. There's that word again.

Toss—This isn't a score either. It means to mix ingredients lightly.

Truss—To tie fowl or meat with skewers and string or needle and thread to hold its shape during cooking.

Now you're ready for the rest of this book. But, please, keep in mind that this book is, basically, one person's opinion, as modified by the rest of the C.A.M.P. staff. There are other methods, ways, preferences—and I'm sure all of them have reason for being. So, keep your eyes and ears open at all times for little tidbits of information that you might be able to pick up in the strangest places.

Don't neglect educational TV cooking shows for more elegant types of recipes. And if you find a better way to do something, or an absolutely fantastic recipe, I'd like to hear about it. And don't hesitate to use a new recipe or a new method just because C.A.M.P., Lady Agatha or mother does it this way. The more you learn, the better the road is paved through that stomach to the heart of your desires.

CHAPTER TWO

When She Reigns, She Pours
(Wines, Liquors, etc.)

Candlelight and wine can raise many a mundane meal into the realm of the sublime. More about the candlelight later on, though; right now we're concerned with the spirit of the meal—the wine.

Wine might be said to be the soul of a good meal. Whether it is used in a marinade or sauce as a basting ingredient, or as an accompanying beverage, it adds a certain something in the way of elegance that cannot be achieved with beer.

Doubtless, you're going to ask what wine you should serve. If you turn to the various books on the problem of wine selection, the astronomical number of answers you're going to get will serve only to confound you further. The best way to determine what to serve, how and with what, is to start out simply, experiment and expand.

There has been, and perhaps always will be, a certain amount of snobbery or P-elegance connected with wine and wine service, but I've found that those who are really in the know are the least snobbish. One particular example is a decorator friend of mine from France, whose shop was invaded one day by a gushing lady customer who had just purchased for him, as a Christmas present, a very expensive bottle of imported French wine. After he had properly oohed and ahhed his thanks and she had left the shop, he told me in confidence that the Gallo winery makes the same type of wine, only better, and at a tenth the price.

So don't be afraid to use cheaper wines—especially if you're on a budget. If you want to, and can afford to buy names, be my guest. But I'll bet most of your guests wouldn't know the difference if they didn't see the label.

First and last are the fortified wines, or ones to which brandy has been added. Ranging in taste from dry to sweet, their alcoholic content is about twenty percent. The drier varieties are usually used as cocktails, the medium-dry varieties may be served with soup, and the sweet varieties are served with dessert, or after meals. The main varieties are Sherry, Madeira, and Marsala, and the labels will generally inform you as to the particular dryness or sweetness of each.

Second, let's consider the dinner wines. Basically there are three varieties—red, white, and *rosé*. Basically, dinner wines are dry, and can be served all through the meal, unless you are set upon the proper wine with the proper course.

The red wines include Bordeaux, Burgundies, Pinot Noir, and Chianti, to mention a few; and are usually served with meat and other full-flavored dishes. Red wines are generally served at room temperatures, but some experts caution, "never above seventy degrees," and some Western tastes dictate that it should be chilled. Try it several ways and see how YOU like it.

Chablis, Rhine, California Sauterne, Riesling, and Moselle are just a few of the white wines you'll find on the market, and generally serve as an accompaniment to an entrée of fish, fowl, or other delicately flavored dishes. They should be chilled, however, and never opened until just before serving.

Perhaps the best known of the rosé wines is Grenache Rosé, but some vintners have taken to calling their products by the English word pink, and now we have Pink Chablis. These, like the white wines, should be served chilled, opened at the last minute—but, may be served with almost anything. In my opinion, they are especially good with pork.

In a class by itself is champagne. Properly, champagne is a sparkling white wine—pink or red champagnes are more properly called sparkling Burgundies. All should be served icy cold and go with anything—so much so that the basic rule is when champagne is served, serve only champagne.

Before we leave our discussion of wines, we should at least mention a few ideas in connection with wine cookery. Nearly all wines can he used in some dish or another. Your question might be, "but which one should I use?" Simple. Use, as an extra added flavoring, the type of wine that you would serve with the dish. Try a dash of red wine over a broiled steak; a spoon of dry white wine in a clear soup: or champagne over a chilled peach half in a sherbet glass. You'll find as you go through this book certain specific ideas for the use of wine in cooking. Use them as a basis, and then as you gain confidence, experiment.

The question now arises, "What are you going to do with your guests until dinner time?" No, Mary, you can't do that—not if you're cooking. There are far too many interruptions. After all, you don't want to burn the roast, or forget to cook the vegetables—and if you already have a cook, you don't need this book anyway. Then again if you do have a cook, he's not going to let you entertain the guests in there! So, you serve them drinks, commonly known as cocktails. There's a helluva word right there.

If your liquor locker is stocked with bourbon, Scotch, gin, vodka, and sweet and dry vermouth, and you have a supply of ice—please don't forget the ice—soda (and perhaps tonic, ginger ale, 7-Up, and cola) in the refrigerator, you are pretty well set for the requests of your guests. If they should happen to ask for something that can't be made from these ingredients, they shouldn't feel too put out, nor should you feel embarrassed, when you answer, "I'm sorry, I don't have it."

After all, you're not expected to be as well-stocked as the local lounge—and chances are, when somebody comes up with a request as just mentioned, they habitually cruise the local bars and are just showing off. For such emergencies you can keep a six-pack in the ice box, and add to your apology, "But I do have some beer if you would prefer." They most likely, then, will choose the beer, or make a simpler request.

The simplest drinks are the **highballs** or "single pass" drinks. For these put four or five ice cubes in a tall glass, pour over at least two ounces of the requested liquor, and fill with the requested beverage.

Most **cocktails** are named according to recipe and can cause very little confusion. For example: Bourbon and water, Scotch and soda, gin and tonic, vodka and seven (referring to 7-Up, of course).

The other drinks you're likely to be concerned with are the **martinis** (both vodka and gin), Manhattans, and Rob Roys. This is where the vermouths come in. You're lucky if your guests specify them "on the rocks," then all you have to do is put an ice cube or two in an old-fashioned glass, pour in the base liquor, add the proper vermouth, stir, and serve.

A nicer way to serve them though is "up"—in a stemmed cocktail glass. In this case the drink is mixed in a pitcher, or if you're working in the privacy of the kitchen when mixing the drinks, almost any container with a spout will do, stirred with ice, and strained into the glass.

For martinis the base is either vodka or gin. Traditionally it is gin, but the preference has so swung over to vodka martinis that in some cities you have to specify "gin" to get a gin martini—otherwise you get a vodka martini. In any case, your proportions should never be more than one part of vermouth to four parts of gin or vodka. There are some hardy souls that prefer no vermouth at all. Serve with a stuffed green olive in the glass. Or a small cocktail onion, which magically changes the drink into a Gibson. And before somebody says, "Ah ha!," use dry or Italian vermouth for this drink.

The **Manhattan** is made the same way as the martini, except that bourbon is used instead of vodka or gin, and sweet vermouth is used instead of the dry. But here you use proportions of one part of vermouth to three parts of bourbon. As Jackie says, "Manhattan drinkers are a different breed." But there are subspecies, and eventually you'll find someone who'll ask for a dry Manhattan, in which case substitute dry vermouth and use less of it.

The **Rob Roy** is traditionally a Manhattan made with Scotch. But so much preference has been made lately for the dry Rob Roy (same rules apply as to Manhattans of this variety) that when your guests request this, it is advisable to ask, "Classic or dry?" It's a good line, too, and simply means "sweet or dry vermouth?"

One word of warning. In the case of the last two drinks, you may run across the rare character who wants his Manhattan or Rob Roy "perfect," in which case you use half dry vermouth and half sweet vermouth, but keep the total amount of vermouth in the same proportion to the base of Scotch or bourbon.

As you expand the variety of liquors and liqueurs in your bar, you'll want more recipes for fancier drinks. One of the best books out, and sometimes called the "Bartender's Bible" is *Old Mister Boston*. It's not expensive and is well worth having.

After dinner, it's nice to retire to the drawing room for coffee and liqueurs, or you may choose to serve them "at table." In any case it's nice to have a selection of three or four at hand, and let your guest choose from among them. Reliable standbys are Cognac (which should always be served in a snifter), Galliano, crème de menthe (the green is more favored), and Drambuie. These latter three should be served in liqueur glasses.

There are many more types available, but these four have particular versatility, as you'll see later on when we get into the preparation of various recipes where liqueurs are specified ingredients. Just to give you an idea, when you're cooking green peas add a dash of crème de menthe, or serve brandy over a peach half.

Eventually you're going to want to entertain more than just a small intimate group at dinner—as sort of a repayment for all those invitations you've received from helpful friends who are trying to get you married off. It's a wise idea, especially if you would like their continued assistance. The easiest (and cheapest) way to provide drinks for such a crowd, usually about twelve or more, is to serve a punch.

This first one is **Fish House Punch**, and Jackie tells me it was one of George Washington's favorites. The recipe serves about fifteen people under normal circumstances.

Dissolve three-fourths cup sugar in one pint lemon juice. Add one fifth of Jamaican rum, one pint of cognac and two ounces of peach liqueur. Stir well, and allow mixture to stand for several hours, stirring from time to time. At serving time, add a block of ice and one quart club soda. One thing more—mix the whole thing right in the punch bowl.

Here's another nice little ice-breaker, if you have an electric blender, and want to live dangerously. It's the **Mollie Hogan**.

In a blender put the juice of twelve oranges and the juice of two lemons, six teaspoons vanilla extract, and six eggs. Mix thoroughly and add one fifth gin (or vodka). Serve one and one-half ounces over ice in a tall glass and add 7-Up to fill. It goes down easy, but gets up slow!

One more, and we'll go on into a discussion of what to serve with all these delightful nectars. This I call **"Either Way"** or **"AC-DC."** You know how it is sometimes when you go to the store and have to make a last-minute substitution because they just sold the last can, box or whatever? Well, that's how this developed.

In a punch bowl (preferably an hour or so before the party) put: two quarts orange sherbet (or ice) or pineapple sherbet (or ice), three fifths chilled sauterne or Chablis, two six-ounce cans frozen orange or grapefruit juice, and one bottle chilled champagne. (No substitutions on this.) Then stand back and let 'em at it.

A word to the wise—if you're planning another activity later on, pour lightly!

CHAPTER THREE
Grand Openings (Appetizers, Canapés, and Such)

When it comes to appetizers, you can be as plain or fancy as your talents and your budget allow. We are trying here, though, to keep the budget at a minimum, and in the case of appetizers that greatly simplifies things.

APPETIZERS & HORS D'OEUVRES

The simplest appetizer, served as a first course at dinner, might be nothing more than a small glass of well-chilled tomato juice served with a lemon wedge.

Another delightful opening to dinner is a shrimp or oyster cocktail, and involves no more than opening a can of shrimp or oysters (or thawing out a frozen package), and serving them in something as simple as a sherbet glass, topped with a prepared sauce.

The present tendency is to eliminate the appetizer course in favor of serving canapés or hors d'oeuvres, so that a number of delicacies that were formerly considered as appropriate appetizers are now classed as hors d'oeuvres. In the main these are rather compli-cated recipes. The beginning cook is going to have enough to do with the main part of the meal, so let's keep things simple.

We must keep in mind that in general cocktails and such are a prelude to dinner—plan accordingly, so that guests are not overfed, or their appetites jaded by the time they arrive at table.

As a suggestion for something light, you might glance back at the section on vegetables and see which ones are edible as raw relishes. Two or three of these, cut to bite-sized pieces and arranged over shaved or cracked ice is a most attractive and delicious prelude. You might even arrange to have a dunk for the vegetables to be dipped in. Here's a real simple one:

To one-half pint sour cream add one tablespoon chili sauce, one teaspoon dry mustard, one grated onion, one teaspoon Worcestershire Sauce, one tablespoon chopped chives, one-half teaspoon salt, and one-half teaspoon cracked pepper. Mix well and chill for one hour before serving as a dunk for raw vegetables.

CANAPÉS

In recent years I've noticed a trend away from the almost tasteless canapé that the Ladies' Aid used to serve at their teas. I'm sure you've seen the kind—those little things made up of different kinds of bread arranged to form stripes, checkerboards, *et cetera*; and all pasted together with some tasteless variety of cream cheese. I'm sure there are few people that will regret their passing. I know I won't hang a black wreath on my door.

Tell me I ain't got no couth—but I like chips and dips. They're easy, they're cheap, they go well with almost anything, and I've never noticed any problem with leftovers.

With the number of crackers (mercy, have you seen the sizes, shapes, and flavors on your grocer's shelf?), toasts, etc., available, you can have a wild time cruising the aisles for the chips part of your dish. And while you're at it, don't forget to consider potato and corn chips as a possibility.

And wild as you may get in your cruising (if it's a good night), don't get too wild on the buying. If your plan is to let your guest do their own dipping, I would recommend no more than two or three varieties. If you plan to spread crackers yourself as a sort of canapé, you may consider as many as eight (keeping in mind your storage space, your time, and your purse).

DIPS

The old standby among dips is the California or onion dip, made very simply by combining a package of dried onion soup mix with one pint sour cream and allowing it to mellow in the refrigerator for an hour or so.

This next one is easy too, but is a little too thick for dipping, so you should serve it with a small knife so your guests can spread their own crackers; or to be a little more elegant, you might spread the crackers yourself in advance, arrange on a tray, and cover until time to serve. Anyhow, all you do is mix one-half pound of liverwurst with one finely chopped onion and one finely chopped green pepper—add a dash or two of tabasco sauce and enough Burgundy wine to soften the mixture sufficiently for spreading.

If you do the spreading yourself, you might want to dress up these canapés by putting a little something on top: say, an anchovy (some people like them), a slice of stuffed olive, a shrimp or a small sprig of parsley. Can you think of anything else? Mary!!!!!!

There are many soft and flavorful cheeses on the market too that you can use in the same way as the liverwurst spread. Simply lay it on and decorate, with any of the foregoing suggestions or even a piece of tomato, a dash of paprika, or a few capers.

Another dip that will offer your guests a contrast in flavors is a minced clam dip—almost as simply made as the onion dip. In a small bowl mix one small can minced clams (well-drained), one teaspoon lemon juice, add one-half pint sour cream, one teaspoon Worcestershire sauce, one-half teaspoon salt, and a dash of pepper. Blend well and set it in the refrigerator to mellow for an hour. This is another one where you let the guests dip their own.

Mary Dugan! Look at that shopping cart. I told you not to get too carried away. We still have an entire meal to go, and we don't want to ruin their appetites. And, besides, I've heard that when a person is overfed they are less inclined to have other appetites. Wouldn't that be a shame?

There will be times when you'll be having a cocktail party without a dinner following, or perhaps just a simple buffet and then you can go hog-wild. But then you'll probably have a whole library of cookbooks, and lots of friendly sisters, tricks, and dolls (dirty, old lecherous ladies). There is the chance that you may want to try your hand at one before this, on a small scale, as a sort of rehearsal for the grand opening.

HORS D'OEUVRES

Many popular hors d'oeuvres are made of meat. We all know why that's popular. Other bases are fish, cheese, eggs, and vegetables. Let's start with a couple of the meat ones.

MEAT HORS D'OEUVRES

Here's one that Alvin Shadow introduced to the three Furies, and even War and Konky enjoyed them. Take a pound of ground round-steak and roll it into little balls about an inch in diameter. Then, in a heavy skillet put one-fourth cup of grape jelly and the contents of an eight- to ten-ounce jar of chili sauce. Add the meat balls and simmer for about half an hour. If the sauce gets too thick, thin it out with a little water. (It's not my recipe, or I might be tempted to add a little wine at this point.) Let it cool down, and then put it into a bowl and let it set in the refrigerator overnight. Reheat to the simmering stage preparatory to serving, and serve in a heated casserole, or if you have it, a chafing dish with a supply of toothpicks on the side, and let your guests spear their own.

At a cocktail party at Casa Gee one of the guests liked these so much, that after her first martini she filled her glass with these little goodies and seemed to enjoy them more than the booze. It's a good thing they had made a super-abundance of them. She was a big girl.

Here's another one of Jackie Holmes' favorites. He takes two pounds of pork and cuts it into strips. (He's not available for questioning now, but I imagine he uses pork steak and that the strips are about one-half inch thick and one-half inch wide.) Then he marinates them in a casserole in a mixture of one and one-half teaspoon salt, one tablespoon sugar, four to five table-spoons soy sauce, two cloves of crushed garlic, two tablespoons honey, two tablespoons sherry, and two tablespoon Hoisin sauce. (There is a note here that tells me that that last is a Chinese vegetable sauce—confidentially, I've never seen it, but maybe if you go to the Chinese section of your present big town, you'll be able to find it there, maybe. I'm sure Jackie would insist that it's a must. He lets it stand in this mixture for at least two hours, and says that overnight is better.) The whole thing is then baked in a 400-degree oven for ten minutes (Make sure your oven reaches the 400-degree mark before putting your pork in. We want to be sure that pork is thoroughly cooked.), then reduce the heat to 250 degrees and continue baking for thirty minutes more.

Served with the proper vegetables, this can make an interesting entrée as well. And there's an additional notation here...if the sauce does not have a rich enough color, you might add a few drops of red food-coloring. Gotta keep things pretty.

FISH HORS D'OEUVRES

Fish hors d'oeuvres are very popular, too, although I could never understand why. I never was able to get past the smell. They are very simple though, and you can always handle the little monsters gingerly and wash your fingertips later in lemon juice. This cuts the odor to some extent.

Any number of fish are available in cans, and all you have to do is drain and serve them. Here's where style shows up. Serve them nicely arranged on a platter, each atop its own little cracker or piece of toast (strip or square), and garnish the platter with lemon wedges and parsley. Very attractive!

The kinds of fish that you'll find available at your market will most likely stagger you if you've never checked this department. Some of the more popular varieties for canapés are anchovies, smoked oysters, smoked salmon, and sardines.

And here's a little idea for a fish spread. Drain oil from one six- or eight-ounce can of sardines, and blend together with one three-ounce package of cream cheese and one teaspoon grated onion, and a dash of Tabasco Sauce. Continue blending while adding suffi-cient Rhine wine to soften for spreading. Serve on toast wedges or crackers.

CHEESE HORS D'OEUVRES

The simplest way, and quite frequently the most attractive way to serve cheeses, is just to arrange an assortment of them on a tray, with small knives for slicing and spreading, and an assortment of cocktail crackers.

You may not be satisfied with this after a while, and will want to try stuffing two-inch lengths of celery with softened cream cheese, or scooping out the tops of those tiny tomatoes and stuffing them with a mixture of blue cheese and sour cream, then topping them off with chopped chives.

Outside of these very few recommendations as to what to do with cheeses in hors d'oeuvres, the best way to get ideas is to pick up those little free recipe books that you'll see from time to time in the liquor and other stores. I wouldn't bother too much with the ones by the cheese counter—the liquor people seem to have much more imagination than the cheese people.

The second best way is to see what other people serve. It's not usually too difficult to see what's been put into an hors d'oeuvre, and even if you should misjudge, who knows, you may turn up with a different and even better recipe.

EGG HORS D'OEUVRES

If you've already used eggs for garnish on another dish, you may not want to consider them as an hors d'oeuvre, but if you do, one of the best is this refugee from the picnic basket. Now I'm just going to give you a basic recipe, and your friends are going to tell you what they put in theirs, as my friends will all be jumping on me (figuratively, of course) and asking me why didn't you use MY recipe. Because, dear girl, I wasn't planning on writing an entire book about deviled eggs.

Hard-boil six eggs, cool, shell, and cut into halves the long way. Remove the yolks and place in a bowl with three-fourths cup mayonnaise, one-half teaspoon dry mustard, one teaspoon chopped chives, and one tablespoon finely chopped parsley. Taste for seasoning and add salt if necessary. Blend well, and stuff into whites and garnish with a dash of paprika. Chill before serving.

VEGETABLE HORS D'OEUVRES

Vegetable hors d'oeuvres, you say? Well, we've already mentioned the raw vegetable platter at the beginning of this chapter—but there are other little tidbits that should be mentioned in passing.

Have you tried stuffed artichoke hearts? You can buy the tiny, canned hearts in the delicatessen section of your super market, then stuff them with a seafood salad. Try tuna salad.

Try the recipe for stuffed mushrooms in the vegetable section of this book—but use mushrooms no bigger than an inch across.

We've already mentioned stuffed tomatoes and celery when we talked about the uses of cheese. But while we're on the subject of vegetables, I think we ought to include one more dip to offer a contrast to the ones already discussed. That is the bean and bacon dip.

Combine one can condensed bean with bacon soup with one-fourth cup chili sauce, two tablespoon minced green pepper, one teaspoon minced onion, and one teaspoon Worcestershire sauce. You may serve it as a dip, or spread it on crackers as canapés.

Eventually you're going to be graduating from this phase of cooking school and trying all sorts of other marvy things like: *Melon au Jambon de Bayonne et au Cointreau*, and Shrimp Rémoulade, or *Pâté de Liégois*—but let's not even consider that here. There are many other suggestions that too require the use of a blender, grinder, or chopper, and if you have only the basic utensils listed earlier in this book, those aren't in your possession yet.

You will encounter people from time to time who will tell you about their favorite ways to prepare eel, squid, and octopus, or snails, rattlesnake, or grasshoppers. If the ideas are not appealing to you, I suggest that you excuse yourself under the pretext that you have to go to the bathroom (which by this time may be no pretext). I only mention them in passing, because if I don't, someone is going to say, "You didn't mention so-and-so."

CAVIAR

One thing that I have glaringly omitted is caviar (which I personally put in a category with anchovies and most of the items listed in the last paragraph). All right, we'll talk about caviar.

First of all, it's expensive—that is, if you want the real good stuff, Caspian Sea sturgeon eggs. And if you should serve caviar, it's just possible that you might have a guest who can distinguish between the real and the imitations. There are many.

Caviar lovers will not appreciate being served the so-called "red caviar" either. These are salmon eggs, and much looked down upon by connoisseurs. To get good caviar you're going to have to be ready to pay from twenty-five dollars to seventy-five dollars (or more) per pound.

Tradition dictates that caviar be served from icy bowls to be spread on buttered thin slices of black bread. All the other gobbledygook came along when caviar crossed the sea.

Finally, caviar is not an hors d'oeuvre to be served with cocktails. It can only properly be served with icy cold dry champagne. I always find that's the saving grace at a party where they are serving caviar. I can at least drink the champagne. (Note: it is also fine to serve caviar in the Russian style with shots of icy cold, as cold as you can get it, vodka. But you don't want to serve too many of these if folks have to walk to the dinner table. VJB)

One more thing—you may not like caviar, and many

of your guests may not like it. Before going to all the expense, it may be well, discreetly, to check your prospective guests' tastes in this regard. Better than having your favorite potted palm smelling like fish two or three days after the party.

Now at the other end of the spectrum of entertaining, it is quite permissible, when you are hosting a small group of intimate friends to do something very simple.

Like, open a can of peanuts and pour them out in a bowl, or a bag of potato chips or corn chips.

And don't forget, if your choice of drinks is beer— and there are many people who honestly enjoy beer (I for one)—it's perfectly proper to serve popcorn or pretzels.

CHAPTER FOUR

The Lady and Her Ladle
(All About Soups)

Soups are beautiful and versatile.

Just imagine yourself on a rainy Saturday afternoon with absolutely nothing to do until he comes over. Then with this thought in mind, you get busy and start working on a homemade soup, and while it's simmering the air is filled with all those delicious smells of herbs and onions and stock. All of a sudden the day seems warmer, and your place seems a little bit cozier.

If you really get inspired, you might fill in some of your time by making some homemade bread. I can almost guarantee that if he is greeted by this combination of aromas upon his entrance, you have him almost halfway down the aisle already.

And versatile? Soup, of course, is very at home on the dinner table. It is equally well-matched with a sandwich to provide a nourishing lunch.

Do you get hungry in the middle of the afternoon? Try a light clear soup—it'll hold you over and won't spoil your dinner.

For breakfast? Yes, even for breakfast. But it's a rare

occasion. Usually when I have the sniffles, I find that a bowl of chicken noodle soup (otherwise known as kosher Penicillin) will warm me up and make me feel a lot better, even if I am alone.

Perhaps you don't feel in the mood for messing around with homemade soup. This is no reason to deny yourself the inherent pleasures. If you've got a can opener, and if you followed the list I gave you of kitchen equipment you have, you need not be left out.

There are many canned, frozen, and dried packaged soups on the market today, most of them good. Your own experiments will tell you which ones are better. We'll try to cover all types in this little chapter.

These prepared soups are good alone, simply following the directions on the can or package, or in combination with each other, and/or with the addition of extra ingredients, like a dash of wine or a spoon of cream (even a spoon of peanut butter).

Betcha weren't ready for that!

BROWN STOCK

One thing I've found is at this point most cookbooks give you a recipe for *Pot au Feu*, which is supposed to give you one meal of soup, meat, and vegetables, and stock left over for making soup. My personal experience has been that when you serve *Pot au Feu*, you have nothing left over—so let's concentrate on the other method of making the basis of most soups, or brown stock. It's actually by far the more economical method, inasmuch as it makes use of all those (well, almost all) leftovers that have been sitting in your ice-box for some time. Plus the other ones that you may have acquired by subterfuge.

Of course, you could just go to your local butcher shop, flatter him a little bit, and get a soup bone maybe—but nowadays it seems what ya gets, ya pays for. So let's get out that bone from last Sunday's roast, and those leftover steaks that the waiter gave you for your pet (you didn't tell him your pet was a parakeet), and if this still doesn't seem like enough, you might invest a few cents at the grocers for enough to give you at least four pounds of meat and bones.

Soup's beginning to sound a little sexy, isn't it?

Now, get out your big cauldron, and toss in your four pounds of meat and bone, and cover with water. I should have mentioned that if any of this meat was raw, you should have browned it first. Anyhow, we'll assume it's all browned, and now you have it covered with water in your cauldron—let it just stand there a half an hour while the water soaks out some of the flavor from the meat.

After the half-hour is up, light the fire and add the vegetables. Necessary ones are: two onions, peeled; three carrots; and two stalks of celery with leaves. It's nice if you can add: one leek, mushroom caps and stems, one tomato, and a *bouquet garni* (this is a little bag you make yourself out of cheesecloth, and fill with a teaspoon of an herb mixture of that name). You can also add those other little leftovers from your refrig-erator, noting these exceptions: don't use broccoli, cauliflower, corn, or beets. And go extremely easy on turnip, parsnips, or cabbage. These are all strong vegetables and tend to hide the hearty beef flavor that we want to come through.

Let your concoction come to a boil and reduce heat, and let it simmer away three to four hours under a lid. Check from time to time to see if the contents are still covered with liquid, and if not, add water. Many cookbooks will tell you to skim off the scum that accumulates at the surface at this point. I say not. This is where many of the vitamins are, and the chances that they'll remain in later are greater if they're not removed at this point.

After cooking, pour the stock through a sieve and allow it to cool, then place it into the refrigerator. When it is cold, the fat will have risen to the top and solidified. Strip it off and throw it away. Underneath you have your brown stock ready to use as is, or you may want to use the following method to clarify it, if you're going to be a perfectionist and are willing to take the time and trouble.

Figuring one egg white for each quart of stock, slightly beat the proper number. Crumple the shell of one egg into the whites and add one tablespoon cold water. Add all of this to the stock mixture and bring to a boil, and allow to continue boiling for about two minutes. Arrange a double thickness of cheesecloth in the bottom of a sieve, dampen the cheesecloth, and strain the stock through it.

LIGHT STOCK

There is very little difference in the preparation of light stock. Use light-colored meats such as chicken or veal, and don't brown it. Use light-colored vegetables and ones bland in favor—no tomatoes.

Vegetable stock is by far the easiest though, unless you have a roommate who is a compulsive icebox cleaner-outer. Simply save the cooking liquid drained off the mild-flavored, light-colored vegetables from your regular daily cooking.

Now I find one trouble in all of this nonsense. Oh, I admit it's nice if you have the time, but usually I decide that I want to have soup and I want it that day. If I go through all this routine of making the stock and all that one day, I find that the next day I'm no longer in the mood for soup. True, the stock can be saved for some time, and if you make it that may well be what you'll do with it. But what about those times when you feel like having soup that very same evening?

Simplicity itself. Bouillon, either in cubes or bottled form. It comes in three flavors; beef, chicken, and vegetable. I prefer the bottled form myself. It's much easier to control the strength of the stock. I've found that with the cubes that once you have it unwrapped, you're more or less forced to use the whole cube.

Now that you know all the ways to make stock, meat and vegetable, dark and light, and know both the long and the short of it, we can start the investigation of what we can do with them.

You may serve your brown stock as beef bouillon

or consommé simply by heating and salting to taste. You may want to add some red or white wine for extra flavor, or a spoonful or two of one of the following for added eye appeal (in any case, allow extra cooking time as specified for the particular addition): rice (twenty-five minutes), noodles (fifteen minutes), finely cut carrots (fifteen minutes), thinly sliced mushrooms (five minutes).

VEGETABLE SOUP

Next there's a recipe for vegetable soup that I know you'll never find the likes of in a can. You'd even be hard put to find it in a restaurant.

Get out your soup kettle again, and put in about six cups of your brown stock. Add two onions, thinly sliced; two thinly sliced carrots; four celery stalks, finely chopped; one finely diced turnip; three thinly sliced leeks (this vegetable used to be rarity in our markets, but is appearing with more regularity now); twelve string beans, cut in small pieces; one-fourth head of cabbage, shredded; two finely diced potatoes; one cup of green peas; and one cup of broken macaroni bits. Add salt if necessary.

Bring all to a boil, reduce heat, cover, and simmer gently until all vegetables are done and their flavors well blended with the broth. This should take about a half an hour to forty-five minutes.

ONION SOUP

Bring six cups of beef broth to a boil while peeling, slicing thin and sautéing four large onions in six tablespoons of butter. Pour the boiling broth over the onions, and add one-fourth cup sherry and salt if necessary. Add one-half cup Swiss cheese, and pour all into a casserole, and place in 350-degree oven for fifteen minutes. Top each serving with a slice of toasted French bread and a sprinkling of Parmesan cheese. Although primarily considered a dinner soup, this is also excellent as a nightcap.

We can treat our chicken stock in the same way as we first treated the beef broth, and serve it simply as a hot broth or bouillon, perhaps adding a little rice or noodles for looks. This is very good on the convalescent's tray. Or we can go on and use this broth to make an excellent vichyssoise.

VICHYSSOISE

In three tablespoons butter, sauté one cup finely chopped white part of leeks and one finely chopped white onion. When they are soft, sprinkle over them one tablespoon flour, and add two cups minced raw peeled potatoes and four cups chicken broth. Cook gently until the potatoes start to fall apart.

At this point most recipes will tell you to push the entire mixture through a sieve, or put it into a blender. This does give a nice even texture, but is not necessary to achieve the proper flavor—so let's ignore the instruction until we can afford the proper equipment, and go on.

Chill the mixture. Yes, Maude, we serve this one cold. And just before we dish it out, we slowly beat in a pint of heavy cream, one tablespoon salt, and a pinch of cayenne pepper. Garnish each cup or bowl with finely chopped chives.

And if ya want to serve it hot...I'll never tell.

Up to now, soup-making has sounded like a fairly complicated operation, what with the intensity of preparing the stock in advance and everything. Fortunately that isn't always the case, and there are a number excellent soups that can be made in an afternoon "from scratch," or with the help of one or more packaged soups.

MINESTRONE

First among these let us consider minestrone. Of course, there are as many recipes for this as there are Italian cooks outside, as well as inside, Italy. But basically it is a naturally thick soup, taking its thickness from its basic ingredients, and not depending on any agents such as flour or corn starch.

Soak one-half pound dried navy beans overnight, drain, then cook them until tender in three quarts of water (about an hour).

Chop two medium onions, two stalks of celery, and three sprigs of parsley, shred one small cabbage, and dice two small zucchini.

Put your best Italian cauldron on the stove, and heat in it two tablespoons of olive oil. Add two cloves minced garlic, brown well, then add the onions and celery, and brown them too. (It's an old Roman custom.) Stir in a half-can of tomato paste, which you have diluted with an equal amount of water, and cook all for five minutes.

Add the remaining vegetables, one teaspoon rosemary, one teaspoon salt, one-half teaspoon pepper, two whole cloves; and stir in the beans with their liquid. Cook slowly for about twenty-five minutes.

Toast a slice of French bread for each serving, and place in the bottom of the serving dish. Pour the soup over the toast, and sprinkle liberally with Romano or Parmesan cheese.

BORSCHT

Another delightful departure from the usual in the way of soups, and another equally simple to make, is borscht. Deep red in color and rich in flavor, this Russian favorite has proven itself around the world.

Put three quarts of water, two pounds of short ribs of beef, three medium onions peeled, and two sprigs of fresh dill in a kettle, and boil for one hour or until the meat falls from the bones. Strain the broth into another pot, save the meat and broth, and discard the rest.

In the meantime, you will have been peeling and cubing three medium potatoes, chopping one small cabbage, and peeling, scrubbing, and quartering three medium beets. Add these now, along with the meat, to the broth.

Pierce a lemon in several places with a fork and add it to the broth too. Now, simmer all until the vegetables are tender. Remove the lemon, and let the soup cool slightly.

Stir in one-half pint sour cream at serving time, and serve in heated soup plates accompanied by dark bread and red wine.

CORN CHOWDER

Now here's a simple one that shouldn't take you more than twenty minutes in all to prepare. Fry four slices of bacon until crisp, drain, and crumble into a large sauce pan. Sauté two medium onions and one sprig of parsley, all finely chopped in two tablespoon butter, and add to sauce pan with one quart milk, one seventeen-ounce can cream-style corn, and salt, pepper, and nutmeg to taste. Combine and heat well without boiling.

What is it? Corn chowder. Wanna make clam chowder?

CLAM CHOWDER

Fry four slices of bacon until crisp, and boil two medium diced potatoes in salted water until soft. When the bacon is done, remove it from the fat and sauté one medium onion, chopped in the fat. Drain the cooked potatoes, save the liquid, and return it to the stove to cook down a bit. Combine the bacon, potatoes, onion, and potato water with contents (including juice) of two small cans minced clams. Bring to a boil, lower heat, and allow to simmer for five to ten minutes. Season to taste with salt and pepper, and add two cups light cream. Heat gently to just below boiling point. Before serving, stir in a pinch of thyme, and dust the top of each bowl with a little paprika.

BLACK BEAN SOUP

Now these next few soups can be made with little more than imagination and a can opener. First of all, we have a variation of Black Bean.

Combine one can of black bean soup with one can consommé and one and one-half cans water. Blend well, heat well, and serve garnished with lemon wedges or slices of hard-cooked egg.

LOBSTER BISQUE

Following are two recipes that successfully combine the flavor of pea and tomato. You don't believe it? Try it. At least once.

Flake the contents of one six-ounce can of lobster meat, cover with sherry, and let it stand while you mix together the contents of two cans of green pea soup and one can of tomato soup with three soup cans of milk. Heat without boiling. Add sherry and lobster and cook without boiling, until the meat is warmed. Serve topped with sour cream. What'll we call it? How about lobster-pea *bisque?*

POTAGE MONGOL

Or simply blend together one can of tomato soup, one can of green pea soup, one-half soup can of water, and one-half soup can of Chablis, and heat to just below boiling. There you are. *Potage Mongol.*

CRAB SOUP WITH BEER

This next one just looks like fun, and when you're asked for the recipe, it's bound to cause a few raised eyebrows.

Simply combine and heat—one can of tomato soup, one can green pea soup, one twelve-ounce can beer, one cup milk, and one six-ounce can crab meat. That's all. Its name? You won't believe this—it's called crab soup with beer.

EGG DROP SOUP

Now here's a little simple something most often encountered in Chinese restaurants called egg drop soup. I'm sure it has a name in Chinese, too, but that language has too many dialects, and I'm not going to worry about it here.

Heat four cups beef or chicken bouillon to boiling, and while stirring dribble in one slightly beaten egg. On contact with the liquid it will spin itself into threads.

At one time I was going to learn how to make *bouillabaisse.* I think a person should know something about even what they consider unpleasant subjects (I happen not to care for fish.) So I got out my cookbooks, and the first paragraph of the recipe, said, "...boil until the eyes fall out of the fish heads."

There will be no recipe for *bouillabaisse* in this book.

By now I'm sure we're all agreed that a steaming bowl of soup is a pleasant sight, and its aroma welcome almost anytime we're hungry. In addition, soup lends itself beautifully to garnishment, many of which are now commercially available, so you don't even have to make your own.

Try any of these for toppings:

Those crisp little cubes of toast called croutons.
Crumbled bacon bits. Especially good on a bean or legume soup.
Popcorn—on tomato soup.
Peanut butter—in mushroom or tomato soup.
Carrot curl—pretty in pea soup.
Thin slice of lemon—good on clear soups, or black bean.
Grated cheese—almost anytime.
Chopped chives or herbs—very versatile.
Sour cream—tomato or consommé.
Oyster crackers—designed for oyster stew, but good elsewhere.

And a host of others!

CHAPTER FIVE

Seafood Aplenty (Fish, Shellfish, and Others)

Now, as all of you who have read this far know, my idea of seafood does not involve a trip to the local fish market. Prejudiced as I am, I have almost always questioned the edibility of the products purveyed by my friendly fishmonger.

I am even appalled by those cooks who recommend that the best way to tell if a fish is fresh is to smell it. Honey, I never smelled a fish in my life that even vaguely impressed me as being fresh. If it swam in on the next wave and landed in my kitchen sink and winked at me, I would still have my suspicions.

Now, of course, I realize that all of this is traceable to a warped childhood. About the only fresh fish that we had available in that part of the country was what the head of the household caught, or what was foisted off on you by other well-meaning fishermen.

I'm told too that I almost choked to death on a fishbone from one of those conniving little monsters when I was two years old. That's perhaps why my attitude has generally been, "You caught 'em, you clean 'em, you cook 'em, you eat 'em."

In all fairness, I must admit that since discovering that there are other fish in life besides those dipped in corn meal and deep fat fried, and two other standbys of my grandmother, salmon salad and tuna salad, my attitude has mellowed somewhat.

I'm sure the whole thing began when I discovered shrimp. This little delicacy was such a revelation to me that I did resolve to go on and try other denizens of the deep, but slowly and in moderation.

So, let's start with these, the least "fishy," and work on to my latest accomplishments.

SHRIMP

I never realized, until I started some research recently, how many different sizes there are of shrimp. Did you know, for instance, that the different sizes of shrimp are numbered, according to how many of a particular size it takes to make a pound. The smallest ones are around "350" and the largest are "-15." That latter means that it takes less than fifteen to make a pound. The big ones, incidentally, are usually called prawns.

There are many available on the market now that are already cleaned, cooked, and quick frozen. These can be either thawed out and used "as are" with cocktail sauce of some sort, or even heated and served in a variety of dishes.

Let's assume that you are going to be a little more ambitious and you want to cook your own shrimp. (In some cases, it's the only way to fly.) You'll find it easier to handle the larger ones, but you'll find that the smaller ones have more flavor. The choice is yours. In any event, allow one pound of unshelled raw or fresh frozen shrimp per two persons if for a main course, and per four persons if for appetizers.

The first thing that must be taken care of is the cleaning of the shrimp. (Personally, this is something that I let the guy at the store do. Pretend he's the hand-somest thing you ever saw and flirt with him a little bit—and he might even do it free.) However, if he's standoffish, you're stuck with the job; so, clothespin on nose, here's how.

Peel off the shell. (It's supposed to come off easily, and I might mention, that if you're serving shrimps as a finger food appetizer, leave the tail on.) Rinse off the grit under cold running water, then, with a sharp knife remove the black vein down the back. They are now ready to cook as desired.

BOILED SHRIMP

Shall we try boiled shrimp? In a kettle, put enough water to cover the shrimp you are going to cook, but don't add the shrimp yet. Instead put in a thick slice of lemon, one medium-sized onion peeled, one stalk of celery, one clove of garlic, one bay leaf, one teaspoon salt, and about three or four peppercorns. Let the water boil with these flavorings in it for about fifteen minutes, then add the shrimp. Lower heat and simmer covered until the shrimps are pink. The time will vary, of course, with the size of the shrimp. As soon as they are pink, however, remove them from the liquid and drain, or they'll go on cooking and tend to become tough and leathery.

Now, they're ready to serve in a tomato-cocktail sauce, a Rémoulade sauce, a Newbury sauce, a Mornay sauce, etc.

SHRIMP CREOLE

With two tablespoons melted butter in a covered skillet, cook one large sliced green pepper, one sliced onion, and one clove of garlic, minced, over low heat until tender. Stir in one can tomato soup, one-third cup water, two teaspoons lemon juice, one-fourth teaspoon salt, and a dash each of pepper and Tabasco Sauce. Add three and one-half to four cups cooked shrimp, and cook about ten minutes more, stirring frequently. Serve over cooked rice. This is especially popular with Southern belles (and gentlemen). One more recipe from the same locale for this little crustacean is Jambalaya—the word itself has a *swingin'* connotation.

JAMBALAYA

Brown lightly one and one-half cups diced cooked ham in two tablespoons oil. Add one cup chopped onion, one-half cup chopped green pepper, and one minced clove garlic, and cook until tender. Add one can tomato soup, one and one-half cups water, three-fourths cup uncooked rice, one bay leaf, one-fourth teaspoon salt, one-fourth teaspoon thyme, and a dash of pepper. Bring to boil, cover, reduce heat, and simmer for twenty minutes, stirring once after ten minutes. Add one-third to four cups cooked shrimp, remove from heat, and let stand covered for about ten minutes. Fluff rice and serve. And as long as you-all's bein' so southern about this, why not whomp up some cornbread to go along with it?

Want to try something a little bit different? Clean your shrimp, and make a single layer of them in the bottom of a buttered pan, season as desired, and dot with butter; then pour in enough liquid, water, or maybe even white wine, to cover the bottom of the pan, and bake in a 350-degree oven for about fifteen minutes.

If you would prefer a broiler method, prepare the same as for baking, but leave the liquid out of the pan. Then cook about three inches below a moderate flame or six inches below a very hot broiler flame. About five minutes should do it.

FRIED SHRIMP

There are two methods of frying shrimp. The simplest, and to my way of thinking, the least unsatisfactory, is just to use enough cooking fat or oil to coat the bottom of the skillet, and toss in the cleaned shrimp, stirring and turning them frequently until done, usually about five minutes.

The other method is the deep-fat method. After cleaning your shrimp, return them to the refrigerator for half an hour to chill. In the meantime make a batter of one cup floor, one cup milk, one slightly beaten egg, one tablespoon melted butter, and one-fourth teaspoon salt. Heat in your skillet sufficient fat to cover the shrimp to a temperature of 350 degrees (this is where a deep-fat thermometer would come in handy, and you might want to add one to your collection of utensils). Dip the shrimp into the batter, and then drop them into the hot fat and cook until a golden brown, about three minutes. It's best not to cook too many at a time so as not to cool the fat. When you serve these, you'd better plan on extras. They don't last long at all.

LOBSTERS

Now, let's talk about lobsters. Personally, I prefer to eat them out at a nice restaurant, or if I simply must have them at home, I'll buy the frozen lobster tails, or even the canned lobster meat. The next few paragraphs should give you a very graphic answer in case you're already asking why.

The best lobsters, I am told, are the ones that weigh between one and one-fourth to two and one-half pounds and are female. I'll leave it up to you to find out how to distinguish the sex of a lobster. I'm not that interested. I've also been told that a fresh lobster should smell good—but I'll be damned if I'm going to get my nose that close to those claws.

Just suppose now that a lobster having passed all its tests with flying colors has finally ended up in your kitchen. What are ya gonna do about it?

The obvious answer is cook it. But...to kill, or not to kill? Obviously, if you're going to serve the lobster it's going to end up dead anyway—but humanitarians have posed the question as to whether 'tis better to allow the beast to suffer the pangs of outrageous fortune before or as it is cooked.

If you're going to broil the little monster, it is necessary to kill and clean it first. For this you need a stout, stiff, and very sharp knife, and one that's on the short side. Hold the lobster firmly on a cutting board, your hands out of his reach, and stab him (some people say one-half inch behind the eyes, and others say where the body and tail meet).

Now the lobster is dead, but unless you know his language and can tell him, the lobster will continue to do everything in his power to convince you that he is just as alive as ever. This, of course, makes the process of cleaning a bit more difficult, and tends to make many people shy away from broiling them. We'll discuss boiling later, and we are better off there inasmuch as we clean them after cooking. In either case the cleaning process is the same. It's just a trifle more difficult when the lobster hasn't been convinced of his demise.

Slit the soft shell on the underside, lift up the tail meat and remove the vein that runs down the back, and find and remove a hard sac near the head. This is called a "lady," don't ask me why.

Now, if you're broiling, the next step is to brush this split side liberally with melted butter, and broil them under a moderate flame at a distance of about three inches, and placed split side up. They should take about fifteen or twenty minutes to cook.

For boiling lobster you need not kill it first. Just have a boiling cauldron with enough water to cover your lobsters, to which you have added a little thyme, a bay leaf, and some salt and pepper. Drop in your lobsters, one at a time, head first, and cook for twenty minutes. During cooking the lobsters will turn from their dark green color to a bright red. After cooking remove from pot, plunge into cold water, and clean as per the instructions for broiled lobster...at least this time he'll lie still.

Figure on one lobster per person and serve with melted butter.

This next recipe is one of the old standbys, and relatively simple once your lobster is cooked. You may use the frozen cooked lobster tails for this (after thawing, of course).

Remove the meat from a large lobster, or lobster tail, and cut into bite-sized chunks. Heat a one-fourth stick of butter in a skillet, and when melted add the lobster and continue heating for about another two or three minutes. The lobster should not change color. Add two ounces (one-fourth cup) sherry (Madeira would be perfect). Heat for another minute, and pour in a mixture of one-half cup cream and two egg yolks. Salt to taste, add a dash each of cayenne and grated nutmeg. Continue cooking over low heat, stirring constantly until sauce thickens. Remove from heat and serve over wedges of toast. This is called Lobster à la Newburg, and can be adapted to shrimps, scallops, oysters, or any delicate meat or fish.

CRABS

Now we turn our attention briefly to that side-stepping denizen of the deep, the crab. The larger variety that you dine upon, and not that dines upon you. Again, I would recommend that you choose your crabs most carefully, preferably from the menu of your best fish house. Improperly cooked, they can be an expensive loss; properly prepared, they are a joy.

There is now such an abundance of frozen and canned crab meat on the market that it is hardly worthwhile to go into a discussion of cooking it—and I think it advisable here only to list one of the favorite ways of preparing the already cooked meat.

Mound shredded crab meat on a bed of crisp greens, and garnish with sliced hard-cooked eggs, tomato wedges, and lemon wedges. Then top all with a dressing made by mixing one cup mayonnaise, one-half cup chili sauce, two tablespoons lemon juice, one tablespoon Worcestershire sauce, a dash each of Angostura Bitters and Tabasco Sauce, and one-fourth teaspoon onion powder. *Voilà!* Crab Louis!

Unless you used shrimp instead of crab—in which case you have Shrimp Louis.

OYSTERS AND CLAMS

Now, of all the mollusks that there are in the sea, you'll probably only ever have to deal with oysters and clams. If you buy the canned variety, you're pretty safe. If, however, you insist on the fresh ones, and they are by far the better, make sure you have a fish merchant with a good reputation who wants to please you, and buy ones that have the shells tightly closed.

One of the favorite methods of serving oysters and clams is on the half shell, raw. If you tell your fish dealer how you plan to serve them, he will most likely be happy to open the shells for you, and then all you have to do is arrange the creatures, six per person, on beds of ice and serve up with a cocktail sauce, or just lemon wedges and salt and pepper. Some people also like a little prepared horseradish on the side.

For those of you whose stomachs are a little too queasy for this introduction to mollusks, you might want to pan-fry them. It's a quite effective way for hiding both the color and texture of these little animals—and paves the way for more daring-do later as you become better acquainted.

You can either have your fish dealer shuck them for you when you buy them, or you may use the canned variety. If you plan on these as aperitifs, I would recommend about six per person, but if you plan on an entrée of clams, figure that a quart of shucked clams or oysters will serve four persons.

Melt a fourth-pound butter in a skillet, then when bubbly, dip each little mollusk in beaten egg, then roll in bread crumbs and drop into skillet. Remove when golden brown, and drain. Serve with salt and pepper and lemon wedges (or if you wish, cocktail sauce).

Simplicity itself is oyster stew. Drain the juice from a pint and a half of oysters, and add to one-half pint milk and one pint cream. Season with salt, pepper, and cayenne. Add oysters and heat to just below boiling, but do not allow to boil. In the meantime prepare the serving bowls by heating them with a tablespoon of butter in each one, until the butter is melted. When all is ready, ladle the stew into the bowls and serve.

FISH

Now we come to that item I've been saving for last. Plain old fish. No matter what it is, tuna, salmon, perch, or whatever when it comes down to basics, it's a fish.

And you can fry it, sauté it; broil it or bake it; boil it or poach it; and it still comes out fish. True, it won't taste or smell the same in every case, or end up with the same texture, but it will still be fish. The amazing thing is that no matter what the variety, almost without exception you can use any of the methods of cooking interchangeably. So much so, that entire books have been devoted on cooking just the different varieties of a particular region of a country.

Basically, unless you live in or near a fishing community, the types of fish that you have available to you will be the steaks and fillets of halibut, sole, cod, etc. that are commonly found in the supermarket, and the inevitable canned tuna and salmon. In this light, then, let us limit ourselves for the present to a brief consideration of these.

For our first recipe let us take two pounds of fresh or frozen fish fillets, cut them in serving-size pieces, and place them in the bottom of a greased shallow baking dish. Sprinkle them then with salt, pepper, paprika, and lemon juice. Make a white sauce (see Chapter Nine) of two tablespoons each butter and flour, one cup milk, and flavored with one tablespoon dry mustard and salt and pepper, and pour over fillets. Sprinkle all with one-half cup buttered bread crumbs and a table-spoon minced parsley. Then bake in a 350-degree oven for about thirty-five minutes. This should serve about six hungry people.

Or try this for halibut steaks. Dissolve two teaspoons salt in one-half cup milk. Dip two one-half-inch thick halibut steaks in the milk mixture, then into one and one-half cups slightly crushed corn flakes, and place on greased cookie sheet. Pour about a tablespoon of melted butter over each steak, and slip into a 400-degree oven for about twenty minutes. Serve with tartar sauce to about four people.

SALMON AND TUNA LOAF

Salmon loaf? Add one tablespoon lemon juice to the drained flaked salmon meat from a one-pound can. Add a cup of white sauce, one-half cup milk, one-half teaspoon salt, one beaten egg, one-half cup chopped celery, and one-half cup dry bread crumbs. Mix well, place in a greased loaf pan, and bake in a 350-degree oven about thirty minutes or till golden brown.

Would you rather make tuna loaf? Then go ahead and use that same recipe that we just looked at, only substitute two six-and-one-half-ounce (or seven-ounce) cans of tuna for the salmon.

TUNA SALAD

Now, for tuna salad, let's take two of those cans of tuna, drain them, and flake the meat into a bowl. We'll add one cup of chopped celery, three chopped hard-cooked eggs, one-fourth teaspoon salt, and a dash of pepper. Mix it all up, then sprinkle the juice of one lemon (about two tablespoons) over the top, then add sufficient mayonnaise to moisten it all well, and mix again. Chill, and serve mounded on crisp lettuce leaves. Garnish with lemon wedges, sliced hard-cooked egg, or ripe olives. For variety you may wish to include four chopped sweet pickles in the mixture.

By proper substitution you can make this into crab, shrimp, or salmon salad.

Now that you're all so well versed on the basics of handling seafood, wouldn't it be fun to try?

CHAPTER SIX
The Chicken Queen (Poultry)

Any discussion of chicken always brings to my lecherous mind the old question that one sweet young thing was said to ask of another, namely: "Tell me, dearie, do you roll your chicken in flour before you brown it?"

Maybe you think she was getting awfully personal, but after all, a cookbook would not be complete without some discussion of the technique of picking out and doing chicken. Some books I've seen have devoted their entire contents to this theme—and some of these were *cookbooks*, too.

All camping aside though, and I'd just as soon not do it in a poultry yard (it gets messy, you know), chicken should be given most serious consideration.

First of all, it's inexpensive (Mother taught me never to use the word "cheap" unless referring to competition). You can feed a hungry male for a third or less using chicken instead of steak.

Second, it's tasty, and there are so many ways to prepare it. There is probably no locale in the world (excluding perhaps the Arctic regions) that doesn't have its own particular method of cooking this most versatile bird.

Third, it is easy to prepare. No longer do we have to go out and catch it, wring its little neck, bleed it, dip it in scalding water, and pluck it. No more do we have the necessity of fouled-up feathers and prickly pin-feathers which have to be singed. Nor do we have the somewhat distasteful task of evisceration.

I find it rather pleasant to be living in an age where I can visit my friendly neighborhood poulter or even supermarket and find the size and weight of chicken I want, already cleaned, either whole, halved, or disjointed, whatever my choice, and all I have to do is take it home and cook it. Delightful!

FRIED CHICKEN

Let's start off then with one of those recipes for a variety of that old-time favorite (Rally Round the Fag and give three cheers for) fried chicken.

One basic rule before we go on. In all the poultry recipes listed here, you can figure about one pound of dressed poultry per person.

So, allowing for the number of persons you are going to be serving, buy an appropriate amount of disjointed chicken (the kind that's marked for frying) at your store. In many places now you can even buy particular parts—thighs, drumsticks, breasts, wings, etc.—instead of the whole chicken.

Allowing one-half cup flour per pound of chicken, place the flour in a paper bag (or what I have found handy for this purpose is one of the one-pound coffee cans, cleaned out of course, that has a tight-fitting plastic lid), along with what looks like enough salt and pepper. Place your chicken parts, two or three at a time, in the bag (or can), and shake until thoroughly coated with the flour mixture, then remove and place on wire rack (or waxed paper or what-have-you). Continue until all parts are coated. Then, starting with the meatier parts first and adding the bonier parts last, brown all in a skillet (one that has a tight-fitting cover) in which there is one-fourth inch of hot cooking fat. Turn each piece two or three times during browning.

Now, add about a one-fourth cup of water to the skillet, and a tablespoon of white wine if you wish, cover tightly, and allow to cook slowly until tender. This can take from thirty minutes to an hour, according to the amount of chicken in the skillet and according to your taste. Personally, I like my chicken well done. Don't we all? (Note: for crispier chicken, uncover after about fifteen minutes. VJB)

STEWED CHICKEN WITH DUMPLINGS

Now let's take a look at another all-time favorite, which of late seems to be overlooked. It takes a little longer to prepare, but is really quite simple. That's stewed chicken, and since I like to do things right, let's make it with dumplings. My mouth waters to think of it.

For six people get yourself a five- or six-pound stewing chicken (you may have to ask the butcher for a stewing chicken, which is an older hen who no longer produces eggs) cut up. Now, in a large sauce pan that has a tight-fitting cover, put three cups of water, one carrot sliced, one onion sliced, and two stalks of celery cut up, and bring to boil. Add chicken and bring to boil again. Cover, reduce heat, and simmer for two to two and one-half hours. Check once or twice during cooking to be sure that liquid does not get too low. When tender, remove chicken and strain liquid. Add enough water to liquid to make two cups, and return to pot along with chicken. Keep hot while you sift together one cup all-purpose flour, two tablespoons baking powder, and one teaspoon salt. Then in a bowl beat one egg, one-half cup milk, and two tablespoons melted butter. Add the egg mixture to the flour mixture and beat until smooth.

Now let's drop this batter on top of the hot simmering chicken in the pot by tablespoonfuls. (Clue—if the spoon is dipped into the hot chicken liquid before spooning out the batter, the batter slides off the spoon easier.)

Now, cover and continue cooking for fifteen minutes. And, Mary, whatever you do, no matter how curious you are, DON'T PEEK. Dumplings are closet queens, and they just won't do justice by your stewed chicken if you interrupt them before they are done. The only excusable way for you to see what's going on inside that pot is for the pot to have a glass lid—and it's been my experience that those things just don't last very long. Anyhow, when fifteen minutes are up, serve piping hot. Yummy!

ROAST CHICKEN

Now, inevitably, someday, you are going to be faced with the prospect of having to roast a turkey. Don't ask me why, but if you ever learn which end of a match to touch to a stove, someday you will be the one elected to do the honors at Thanksgiving or Christmas. Just thank your lucky stars and stripes that in this country we are not prone to celebrate these holidays with something more exotic, like duck or goose.

So, in light of this prospect, we might as well have what you could call a small dress rehearsal—something to get you prepared for the big day when it comes.

Roast chicken is what I'm rambling on about. And it can range in size anywhere from two to four and one-half pounds. If you should want to try something a little larger, and still stay out of the turkey line, get a capon, which can go up to six or seven pounds.

Anyhow, once having our bird, our next consideration is the stuffing. Here is a basic recipe, which should be adequate for a four-pound bird. If yours is not four pounds, adjust your proportions accordingly.

Combine four cups dry bread cubes, three tablespoons chopped onions, one and one-half cups chopped celery, one teaspoon salt, one-fourth teaspoon pepper, one-fourth teaspoon poultry seasoning, and one-third cup melted butter. Toss gently while adding sufficient chicken bouillon or broth to moisten. (If you don't want to go to all this trouble, there are packaged mixes on the market.)

Next, make sure that you have removed the package

of giblets from the inside of the bird. (I assume you're going to get the already dressed variety, rather than the dress it yourself type.) Rub the inside lightly with salt. Fill the cavity and neck opening with the stuffing, and pack *lightly*. This stuff expands during cooking. Now close the cavity with skewers or poultry pins. (These are generally available; if you're going to be cooking much poultry, they're a wise investment. Instructions for their use are on the packages.) Pull neck skin back over stuffing and fasten skewers or pins to bird's back.

With a long cord, tie the ends of legs together; bring cord from legs down around tail, drawing legs down close to body, and tie legs to tail. Bend the tip ends of wings backward so they are held against the back of the bird. Tie in place if necessary. Grease the bird lightly with soft butter, and sprinkle with salt and pepper. Place the bird breast side up on rack in open roasting pan, and place a piece of aluminum foil tent fashion over the breast—loosely, so heat can circulate around it. Roast in a 350-degree oven. Approximately thirty minutes per pound for chickens under four pounds, and twenty-two to twenty-five minutes per pound for those over four pounds. When the leg moves easily, the chicken is cooked. Or test by puncturing the thigh joint with a fork. If the juice runs red, the chicken is not yet done. It is cooked when the juice is clear. Then remove the skewers, pins, and cord and transfer to a large platter, and let it rest for at least ten minutes. And use your pan juices meanwhile to make a scrumptious chicken gravy.

TURKEY

Now, let's talk about that bigger bird—the turkey. Your basic preparation is going to be about the same, except that in most cases you're going to have to make a lot more stuffing. One word of caution—important— if you have a small, apartment-type stove, make sure the bird you're going to cook isn't too big for the oven.

We'll have to cook the turkey at a lower temperature, too. Say about 325 degrees and according to the following chart:

4 - 8 lbs—3¼ - 4½ hrs.
8 - 12 lbs—4½ - 5½ hrs.
12 - 16 lbs—5½ - 6½ hrs.
16 - 20 lbs—6¼ - 8½ hrs.
20 - 24 lbs—8½ - 10½ hrs.

You may test for doneness the same way you test the roast chicken, but perhaps a better way would be to insert a meat thermometer. It should register 165 degrees when inserted in the stuffing, or 200 degrees if inserted in the flesh part of the thigh.

If the turkey stands about twenty minutes before carving, the carving will be easier—and of course, don't forget to serve turkey with cranberry sauce.

Now, I have a cookbook at home that purports to be an everywoman's type cookbook, and under poultry they have recipes for every conceivable fowl dish you can imagine. I will concede that someday you may have an occasion to cook duck—perhaps to impress someone. It's hardly what I'd consider an economical dish, but I sincerely hope that the only place you'll come in contact with such items as goose, Guinea hen, pheasant, squab, or quail will be on the menu of a fine restaurant. Even in the matter of duck, however, I shall trust that by the time you're ready to tackle such an operation, and that's exactly what it can be—some gourmets refer to it as a ritual, and indeed need a small altar of sorts laid out in advance with all the necessary sacrificial materials. (It's quite a performance and usually requires the help of at least one assistant— perhaps acolyte would be a better word.) Well, as I started to say and got sidetracked, by then you'll have more advanced guides to the culinary arts, and more of the necessary equipment.

SUPRÊMES DE POULET AU VIN

However, I do want to give you one more recipe before leaving this discussion of poultry. Let's get fancy and call it by a French name. How about *suprêmes de poulet au vin?*

In three tablespoons melted butter, sauté one minced onion. Add two chicken breasts, halved, and brown well. Heat one-half cup brandy, pour over chicken, and ignite (set fire to it, honey, that's what I said, and be careful of your do).

Mix one can cream of mushroom soup, one-half cup dry sherry, one-fourth teaspoon garlic powder, and one-fourth teaspoon tarragon. Transfer chicken to a baking dish (casserole, in this case), cover with this mixture, cover the dish, and bake in a 350-degree oven for thirty minutes or more. Serve nested on noodles almondine. (I would recommend the packaged noodles almondine for this latter. It's a hell of a lot easier, believe me.)

Now that you know what to do with it, go get 'em, Gert!

CHAPTER SEVEN

You and Your Meat (Beef, Veal, Lamb, Pork, & Others)

Maude was just telling me the other day that when she used to live back in Salem they had a saying— Heaven sends us good meat, but the devil sends cooks. She also added that she has seen some "devilishly good meat."

Well, let's face it. Everyone, at some time or other has drooled over a good piece, whether it be at the dining table or elsewhere. And when it's been properly prepared, we all know it can be divine. But let's not put the cart before the horse. Before we can do anything about it, when we feel the desire for good meat we must set out in the appropriate direction to get it. Pick it up—oops!—I mean go out and get it home.

If you're fortunate enough to have a good butcher shop, you may pay a little more for your meat than you would at the supermarket, where they have everything wrapped in plastic nowadays, but you should get better meat. Especially if that handsome devil behind the counter knows you'll send him more customers if his meat is good, and if he tries to pass off inferior material, that you won't hesitate to come in at the rush hour, brandishing a limp piece of meat in your hand and reading his beads at the top of your lungs. Good beef should be properly aged. Your butcher knows this, only he refers to it (and get this, Mary) as well-hung!

However, lacking a good butcher, you are pretty much left on your own, and maybe we can give you a few hints on how to pick out a good piece from those plastic-wrapped ones in the supermarket.

I'm sure you've all seen those funny purple markings on the fat side of the meat from time to time. Well, anyhow, they're inspector's stamps, not tattoos, and generally indicate the quality of the meat. There are four categories in common usage: prime, choice, good, and commercial. Prime grades are usually bought up by the quality restaurants and hotels, and rarely, if ever, does it find its way even to the butcher's case. Choice is about the best you'll ever have a chance to buy, and in the case of most steaks and roasts that's what you'll want. Good is an "adequate" grade, but lends itself only to the slower methods of cooking, inasmuch as it does not have the natural tenderness of the better grades. But, if you see the stamp that says "commercial," forget that cut and pick out something else.

I'm sure too, that if you check among your friends, that you'll discover that certain markets or chains have a better reputation than others regarding the quality of their meats. Remember: when buying meat, price is often a guide to quality—not always, but most frequently. It's seldom, if ever, that you'll find a good bargain piece of meat.

Now, we'll get around to what kinds of pieces (cuts) to get in a moment, but first, let's talk about the seven basic methods of cooking meat.

ROASTING

First of all there's roasting, a method usually applied to all larger cuts of beef, veal, lamb, or pork; but it should be a tender cut. Season by rubbing with salt and pepper and garlic and other herbs as desired. Place the fat side up on rack in open roasting pan. If you have a meat thermometer, insert it into the thickest part of the meat, but in such a way that the bulb does not rest on the fat or touch the bone. Set oven temperature at 325 degrees. Add no water and do not cover. Roasting is a "dry heat" method of cooking. If water is added or the pan covered, you are pot-roasting. Place roast in oven until done. When's that? We'll come to that later.

BROILING

Next we have broiling, and that will include charcoal broiling, which we will of necessity treat separately. Right now we'll concern ourselves with the kitchen type of broiling, under gas flame or electricity. Turn your oven regulator (I sincerely hope you have one— I've seen ranges in efficiency apartments that don't) to broil, and preheat the broiler. This heats the rack and produces those little criss-cross scorch marks that say, "broiled." Then adjust the height of the broiler so that the meat will be two to three inches from the heat; and the thicker the meat, the further from the heat it should be. Broil until the top side is thoroughly browned, season with salt and pepper, turn over, and brown the other side. How's that for a neat trick? Season and serve. We'll talk about the timing for varying degrees of doneness in a minute.

PAN-BROILING

Pan-broiling is another favorite method for cooking smaller steaks, chops, and other tender cuts of meat. In fact, one confused New York housewife who had a number of friends who disagreed vehemently on the proper method of cooking steak had a "steak-tasting" party, at which each of the dissenters was given an opportunity to prepare steak the way he or she thought best, then all of the guests were invited to sample the results. This method proved to be the most popular with her guests.

Well, it's one way to entertain and get out of doing the cooking. But so that you can add pan-broiling to your accomplishments, let's see how it's done. An aluminum fry pan is especially good for this method, although an iron skillet will do. Place it over medium-high heat until hot enough. A simple way to tell when the proper temperature is reached is to place a piece of white paper in the bottom of the pan, and when the paper turns a golden brown, the pan is ready.

Remove the paper and throw in a bit of salt to lightly cover the bottom of the pan, and toss your steak, chop, or what-have-you on top. It will stick at first, but the searing juices will soon release it as it browns. When it is brown on the one side, turn and brown the second side. Remember, do not add water, do not cover. Cook until degree of doneness desired is obtained, season, and serve immediately.

PAN-FRYING

Pan-frying is the word for the next method and it's done in a fry pan on top of the stove much the same way as Pan-broiling, except that you use about two tablespoonfuls of fat. A variation is to use butter, in which case it is called sautéing.

This latter is a favorite method of preparation, especially among the French and the Italians, and although many Americans think it a crime to cook steak by this method, some cuts like tenderloin, filet mignon, and tournedos can use the extra lubrication.

Other uses of this method are for meat that has been pounded, cubed, scored, or ground, or meat that has been breaded. In any event, after heating your pan to the proper treatment, add the fat (or butter), no salt this time—then proceed exactly as for pan-broiling.

DEEP FAT FRYING

Deep fat frying is usually reserved for breaded meats or croquettes (that's not a wicket game), and is a lot easier if you have a French fryer, or at the least a deep fat thermometer. I usually judge the fat to be hot enough if it bubbles vigorously when the meat is dropped in—the temperature should be between 300 degrees and 350 degrees, and at least one-half inch deep. If your fryer is deep enough, of course, you will use enough to cover the meat. In the shallower fat, turning will be necessary to properly brown all sides. In fat to cover, no turning will be necessary. Best results are obtained when only a few pieces are fried at one time. When pieces are done, drain excess fat on paper towels.

The fat, if strained, cooled, and stored in the refrigerator, may be used again.

POT ROASTING

Pot roasting, a term used interchangeably with braising, is an excellent method for cooking the less tender cuts of meat. And even some of the tender cuts, like pork and veal steak, chops and cutlets are enhanced when cooked by this method.

First, brown the meat on all sides, and in some cases you may dredge the meat in flour first, as in pan-broiling. Then season, add liquid (water, wine, or whiskey—have a ball), cover, turn heat to low and cook until tender. A tough piece of meat—bottom round beef steak, for instances, or a pork steak, can take an hour.

STEWING

And seventh and lastly: how to cook in water, otherwise known as *stewing*. Brown meat on all sides and cover with water or stock (liquid need not be hot). Season with salt, pepper, herbs, and vegetables; cover and simmer at a low temperature until tender. You would normally do this with, say, a chuck roast, and don't be in any hurry; depending on size, it will take at least an hour, but better plan on two.

The browning can be skipped in this method; however, it helps to develop flavor and improves the color.

In stews use one-inch cubes of meat and flour before browning. Then proceed as usual, except hold back on adding the vegetables until about one hour before cooking time is completed—but more about stews in another chapter.

BEEF

By far the most popular meat in this country is beef, and the most popular cut, steak. Sit down, Grace, I'm talking about what goes on your table. Even here you have a wide range of choices, both quality-wise and price-wise. You'll find that the most expensive cut is usually the porterhouse, and undoubtedly one that you'll serve only on the most ultra-special occasions, since to really impress with this number it should be at least two inches thick, and that's a lot of meat.

The T-bone is not as big around as the porterhouse,

but should be cut as thick. It lends itself better to individual servings, but I might say, most generous ones. This is not the steak for a light snack.

The tenderloin refers to the filet of the loin—the part that forms the small, tender, inner portion of the loin cuts. From it are cut some of the fancier slices, such as filet mignon, chateaubriand, and tournedos. By weight it is the most expensive, but since there is no bone, it is on a par with the porterhouse as far as actual cost is concerned.

Finally, when we come to the sirloin, we get a break in price. There is a higher percentage of bone, but when cut thick it makes an excellent meal for a group. The end of the loin provides us with the cuts known as Delmonico or club steaks. The so-called strip sirloin (on the West Coast they call it New York cut) is actually a porterhouse with the filet (and sometimes the bone) removed.

About the only one left that can actually be called a true steak is the rib steak—and the only one that can be cooked satisfactorily like the rest of the above. The remaining "steak" cuts—rump, chuck (from the shoulder), round (from the hindquarters), and flank (also called London broil)—are best prepared by other methods.

The most favored method of preparing the more popular cuts is probably broiling, and probably the most practical since the broiler can accommodate a greater number of cuts than can the fry pan necessary for pan-broiling (which our New York housewife's friends preferred); and sautéing (preferred in France and Italy). In summer, however, midsummer madness changes the trend to charcoal broiling, and this must not be overlooked.

BARBEQUING

Gone at last are the days when we have to crumple up a month's accumulation of newspapers to dry out the kindling wood while trying to get it to catch fire. Gone, too, is the agonizing wait while the cool-burning wood slowly makes progress in igniting the stubborn charcoal. I have seen the days when I thought it would be easier to set ablaze a bar of pig iron by rubbing two sticks together than to get the charcoal broiler lighted.

Now the barbeque pit is mechanized. We have electric fire starters, and special fluids we can sprinkle on the coals to speed our efforts. As a result, we have a superabundance of backyard chefs. If you don't believe me, have a barbeque sometime and you'll be amazed at the amount of free advice you'll get—and take my advice (I give it away, too), Mary, and if He wants to take over in the charcoal department, let him. Relax for a change.

Even with all this progress in the pre-civilized art of making meat more edible, allow time to properly prepare your fire. After your bed of coals has lighted, allow it to burn until it is covered with a fine layer of white ash, and you can perceive a bright red glow underneath. There should be no flame left. Flame under a steak will serve no other purpose than to burn it. Adjust the grill's height so it is about four or five inches over the bed of coals and you're in business.

Put your steak on the grill till it's done on one side, turn, and finish cooking and remove. When cooking by this method, it is best to use tongs for turning the meat—this prevents leaking out any juices that have been sealed in by the searing process, and helps prevent small grease fires that might flare up as a result. But just to be on the safe side, keep a small spray bottle of water handy to quickly quench these fat-in-the-fire flare-ups.

How long should you cook a steak? I was afraid you'd ask that question. This depends upon so many factors (type of fuel, disposition of your stove or barbeque pit, type of skillet, if any, thickness of steak) that a direct answer is difficult. Most of all, it depends on your own personal or local definition of rare, medium, or well-done. Let's put it this way: if your steak is one and one-half inches thick, under most conditions cooking it from four to five minutes on a side will produce a rare steak. Take it from there and judge according to thickness, heat, and personal preferences.

ROAST BEEF

After the basic work with steak, and it's a good jumping off point for a beginner, we can graduate to roasts. Although the overall cost of a roast is higher, you'll find that they go further, lasting sometimes for days and days, and ending up in sandwiches, soups, stews, hashes, etc.

Actually, only two roast cuts of beef are usually suitable for the true roasting or dry heat method of cooking. They are the rib roast and the sirloin roast. Rump roast can be cooked by this method, but good results are only assured if the grade is prime. Rump roasts generally lend themselves better to the pot roasting or braising methods of cooking. Chuck and round roasts are other cuts which benefit from slower, longer cooking.

A meat thermometer is probably a very wise investment by the time you get around to trying roasts. It's the one sure way of testing for doneness. Most experts agree that rare beef should have an internal temperature of 140 degrees, medium a temperature of 160 degrees, and well-done, 170 degrees. But I've yet to find two of them to agree on exactly, or even approximately, how many minutes per pound a roast should cook to reach that temperature, even when they're using identical methods and cooking temperatures.

The favored temperature for most roasting is 325 degrees, and trying to strike a happy medium that won't overcook your meat, cooking time should be eighteen or twenty minutes per pound for rare roast, twenty-two to twenty-five minutes per pound for medium, and twenty-seven to thirty minutes per pound for well-done.

In the case of the pot roast, it is better to depend on a minutes-per-pound type of timing, and allow anywhere from thirty minutes to an hour per pound. The tougher cuts are better when cooked longer and to a greater degree of doneness. If you happen to be using a more choice grade of meat or a tenderer cut, you can utilize the lesser cooking time.

One thing I nearly forgot to mention, and it's most important. When you buy your meat, you should consider at least a half-pound per person. After all, meat will be the center of attraction upon almost any occasion.

GROUND BEEF

Then I want to mention a few things about ground meat before we leave off on our discussion of beef. It's usually wisest to skip over those packages labeled hamburger. The extra price you pay for ground round, or if you prefer a higher fat content, sirloin or chuck, is well worth the extra dividends you get. The "hamburger" is generally scrap meat with a very high content of fat and gristle which only cooks away and results in a type of false economy. Ground meat, of course, can be made up into patties and cooked in any of the ways we used with steak, or can be made into a tasty meat loaf like this one.

Marinate (that means soak) two pounds ground beef in one cup red wine for at least an hour, or longer, even overnight, if possible. Chop two medium onions, one small green pepper, two stalks of celery, and mince one clove of garlic, then sauté all in four tablespoons butter. Add to the meat along with two-thirds cup bread crumbs (available in packages), one-half cup chopped parsley, one and one-half teaspoon salt, one and one-half teaspoon dry mustard, and one-fourth teaspoon each of ground black pepper, nutmeg, thyme, ground cloves, and cayenne, and two whole eggs. No, dearie, not the shells, just the whole insides.

Now, plunge your clean hands into the whole mess and mix *thoroughly*—a spoon won't do for this job. Shape into the form of a loaf and place in baking dish. Over the top spread or pour a mixture of one-half cup catsup, one-fourth cup wine vinegar, two teaspoons Worcestershire sauce, one minced clove of garlic, one tablespoon grated onion, one-half teaspoon chili powder, and one teaspoon prepared mustard (the wet kind). Put the pan in a 350-degree oven and bake forty-five to sixty minutes.

VEAL

Veal, while not as popular a meat as beef, is still quite delicious in the opinion of many people, including me. However there are those, some of whom may never have tasted it, who will swear up and down that they can't stand veal. Now, with some of these people you could serve it to them and call it rabbit filet and they'd never know the difference, but there are those who CAN tell. So, to be on the safe side, check the preferences of your guest list before you serve veal.

The Italians are very fond of veal, and one of the most famous veal specialties they have is actually very simple to prepare. So, if you like to be continental why don't you camp it up and try veal scaloppini. The name, unlike the names of many European dishes, does not come from the sauce used on it, but from the cut of the meat. We shall use thin slices of veal from the shank, about six, which is enough usually for four people. These slices of veal shank are called scallops, hence, scaloppini.

First, dust your veal slices with about six tablespoons of flour in all, then set them aside while you melt four tablespoons butter in a heavy fry pan, and cook in this butter three thinly sliced medium onions and one clove minced garlic until they are yellow. Add one cup boiling water and two bouillon cubes (beef), and stir until dissolved. Add one teaspoon dry mustard and three teaspoons paprika, stir, pour into bowl, and set aside.

Melt four more tablespoons butter in skillet, add floured veal and brown on both sides, pour the onion mixture over the meat, and cook over low heat for thirty minutes. Stir in one cup of sour cream, bring to boil, remove from heat, arrange on platter, and serve.

LIVER

While on the subject of veal, we should take a look at its liver, usually referred to as baby beef liver. If you don't eat liver at all, you might as well skip over this next paragraph, but if you're one of those who eats liver either because you like it or because it's good for you, you might as well know how properly to prepare it.

When you buy the liver in the first place, get it in one-fourth or one-half inch slices. Use it the same or the very next day at the latest. Half an hour before cooking time, try marinating it in wine vinegar or milk, then dredge each slice in flour, and set aside while you melt a few tablespoons of butter in a fry pan; then sauté one or two medium thinly sliced onions until they are yellow. Add the liver, brown quickly on one side, turn, season with salt and pepper, and when brown on the other side, remove from fire, and there you are. Liver and onions!

VEAL CHOPS

Veal also has many cuts similar to beef; however, veal being from a considerably smaller animal, those cuts of beef referred to as steak are, in the case of veal, referred to as chops. Roasts are pretty much the same, except that they should be cooked either rubbed well with fat or with a few strips of bacon on top of them, since veal is a very lean meat and needs extra lubrication. You know how that can be. You can generally cook veal at a slightly slower temperature as well, around 300 degrees, but a little longer. Internal temperature should be 170 degrees. Veal should always be well done.

PORK

Next we'll consider the second most popular meat in the country (oh, all right, have it your way, the third)—namely, pork. First of all, I cannot stress too much, pork must always be cooked well-done. I like my beef bloody, but when it comes to pork, I want it cooked clear through.

PORK CHOPS

Pork boasts many versatile cuts. Chops, of course are one favorite, ham (from the rear leg) and picnic ham (from the shoulder) probably run a close second—and almost everybody likes bacon. And barbequed spare ribs. Mmmm. Don't forget fresh roast pork. We'll get into a specialty dish in that regard in a moment.

Chops will most likely be your main consideration, outside of bacon. If you can, get them from three-fourths to one-inch thick. Any thinner than that and you have a very small chop. Any thicker and they take forever to cook. Chops should be browned quickly on one side, then turned quickly, and the heat reduced and cooked slowly, turning again if necessary until they are a light gray color all the way through. Absolutely no pink at all, ever. How long is it going to take to cook these thick chops? Honey, allow at least an hour.

PORK ROAST

And now the specialty recipe. Hi-C.A.M.P. would never forgive me if I left out this recipe for crown roast of pork. For this one you do need the cooperation of a butcher. He will form the crown from a rack of ten or twelve ribs for you; then what you do is take it home, season it with salt and pepper, and put it in your roasting pan, bone ends up. Be sure to put something on the ends of the bones to prevent their charring, such as a piece of salt pork or bacon. Now, make a batch of stuffing, like the one we made for roast chicken, and put it in the middle of this. Place your roast in the oven, which should be preheated to 325 degrees, and roast until done, allowing forty-five minutes per pound. If you have a meat thermometer, the interior temperature of a pork roast should be 185 degrees when properly done.

To serve, remove fat from bone ends, and decorate them with paper frills, stuffed olives, crabapples, or steamed prunes.

LAMB

Similar racks of ribs from veal and lamb can be treated the same way, but as I've mentioned before, consider your guests before serving either of these meats. Yes, that goes for lamb, too—it's another one of those no-I-never-tasted-it-but-I-still-don't-like-it meats.

I don't know if this stems from the days when a typical recipe for preparing a leg of lamb might run: take ye legge of lambe and letteth it laye on ye sinke untill it stynketh.

No, thank you. If it stynketh, it's one piece of meat Lady Agatha's not taking home in the first place. And if it should get that way in the refrigerator, heaven help Prissy.

I much prefer to buy my "legges of lambe" the day before I cook them—and I don't lay them on the sink.

It goes into my refrigerator until I'm ready to prepare it.

Then, wipe the entire leg with a damp cloth. Do *not* remove the thin papery skin (called a fell) from the leg.

Rub the entire surface with the cut side of a clove of garlic—your fingers may have an aroma for a while after this operation, but the final result is worth it. Now, rub with salt and pepper as well. Place the whole leg, fat side up, on a rack in your roasting pan and place in an oven preheated to 325 degrees. Allow thirty-five to forty minutes per pound for a smaller (four to six pound) roast, and thirty to thirty-five minutes per pound for a larger (six or seven pound) roast. Note: the smaller the roast, the longer the cooking time per pound. Add no water (remember, that's pot roasting), and do not baste.

Lamb is usually accompanied with mint jelly or mint sauce, although it is not necessary. Green peas make an excellent accompanying vegetable to a lamb entrée, but don't let these suggestions limit you. The Armenians, for instance, enjoy fixing their lamb with eggplant.

Lamb has many other equally delectable cuts: chops, ribs, etc., and these are cooked much in the manner of the same cuts from veal—more well done than beef, but not necessarily as well done as pork, depending upon the taste of the individual.

SPECIALTY MEATS

There are a few other specialty items, called variety meats, which do bear at least honorable mention in this chapter. However, the preparation of them is in some cases quite involved, and unless you are determined to become a gourmet chef, they are better left to the preparation of professionals in the better restaurants.

I'm talking, of course, about those inner, and sometimes much maligned cuts, such as tongue, brains, tripe, sweetbreads, heart, kidney, and the most uncommon on the meat counter, "fries." These latter are really the nuts.

Oh, God! I'm almost guilty of calling down the wrath of Jackie Holmes on me. He told me not to forget to tell you about his recipe for stuffed pork chops on page seventy-four of *Sex and the Single Gay.* There I've told you—and I must admit, it is good.

CHAPTER EIGHT
Which Came First? (The Egg and Related Items)

The simple little egg is probably the most prominent single food in our diet today. It may appear as an egg only infrequently, but it has so many other uses that we must learn to treat it with respect. It is included as one of the ingredients in pies, cakes, puddings, omelets, sauces, soufflés, salads and salad dressings, sandwiches, stuffings, batters, pancakes, and bread. This I'm sure, is only a few of the ways in which we daily encounter the egg. Eggs are also a very rich source of protein, iron, and vitamins. Before the days of cholesterol and polyunsaturated fats, it was recommended that one egg per day, at least four per week, be included in the diet.

Let's take a look at the basic ways we can fix them, and then a brief glance at the variations.

SCRAMBLED EGGS

First of all, scrambled. The nice thing about scrambled eggs is that you don't have to be so damned careful when you're cracking them open. Our minds relieved of this, we heat a bit of butter in a skillet, add the number of eggs necessary, two or three per person (but not too many for the skillet, Mary), and cook over medium heat, stirring frequently, but not constantly. We want a mixture of gold and white—not just one blur of light yellow.

Some people like their scrambled eggs still on the slightly liquid side, in which case remove them from the Pan as soon as they are the right consistency; some people like them a little bit harder (eggs, that is), and you don't have to rush so about getting these out of the pan. But as long as the eggs are in the pan, they will continue to cook, so when they get to a particular stage that you want, get them out fast. Then season to taste and serve.

FRIED EGGS

There are some things I like to do the easy way, and one of them is fried eggs. For them I use a skillet that has a tight-fitting cover. I put a little butter in the skillet (some people like bacon grease, but I prefer butter), melt it, then gently break the eggs into the pan one at a time. When the whites are set and the edges of them cooked, I add about a teaspoon of water per egg, and quickly put the cover on and cook until done. (Sometimes I substitute wine for the water. It adds a most interesting flavor to the eggs.)

Doneness is here again a matter of personal choice. For the sunnyside-up people, you would remove the lid almost as soon as you put it on, and serve; for the over-hard people, they would have to cook a while until the yolks were set as well; then there's always those in-betweens. This method of cooking eggs is called basting, and avoids the necessity of using a spatula to turn the eggs in what is a rather cramped space, and at the same time avoids the possibility of breaking the yolks in such a turning.

SHIRRED (BAKED) EGGS

Shirred (or baked) eggs are rather uncommon. Perhaps it's because they require individual baking dishes called ramekins. If you see them on a menu, or if you find a buy in the thrift store, you might want to know how they're done. So, here's how:

Grease your little baking dishes, preferably with butter. Slip in your eggs, one per dish (two at the most, if you have bigger dishes or smaller eggs). Season with salt and pepper, and add a bit of melted butter. Bake in an oven preheated to 325 degrees for about twenty minutes. Result? Shirred eggs.

One variation would be to put about one-fourth cup of chopped, cooked spinach per ramekin, and nest the egg in it. Then add about a tablespoon of cream instead of the extra melted butter.

BOILED EGGS

Now, the boiled egg. Some cooks say, "There ain't no such animal." I say, "Of course, there is—but it's not necessarily the best way of preparation." Eggs are delicate and should be literally *coddled.* And here's how we do it. Place your eggs, whole, in cold water to cover completely. Place the pan over medium heat and bring to a boil. Lower the heat immediately, and cook the eggs slowly two to five more minutes for a soft-cooked egg, depending again on the degree of softness desired. Leave the eggs in fifteen to twenty minutes for a hard-cooked egg. If the hard-cooked eggs are to be used cold, plunge them immediately into cold water before removing shell. This prevents dark rings from forming around the yolks.

Point of interest here. At the point where the water begins to boil, the eggs are said to be coddled, just in case Miss P. Elegant wants hers that way.

POACHED EGGS

For next to last, I've saved the method referred to as poaching. This is a method of preparing eggs, no longer in the shell, but in hot water. The trick is to keep the white from going all over and forming what looks like a bridal veil in your cooking vessel.

Grease your skillet (preferably a stainless steel one for eggs, and again with butter), and add enough water to float the eggs you'll be cooking, along with a one-half teaspoon of salt per quart of water. Heat to boiling and reduce heat. When boiling action has stopped, break an egg into a sauce dish, lower gently into and toward the side of the skillet, then do it individually with each egg.

The reason for all this care in introducing the eggs

into the skillet, is, of course, to prevent the dissipation of the white. A better method might be, though, to put muffin rings or large round cookie cutters into the skillet and drop the eggs into these. Howsoever you cook them, and to whatever degree of doneness desired, when cooked, remove them one at a time with a slotted spoon or pancake turner, drain, and serve on buttered toast.

A very popular variation of poached eggs is Eggs Benedict. For this, split and toast an English muffin for each guest. Lay a thin slice of broiled ham on top of each slice. Top each with a poached egg, and pour Hollandaise sauce over all.

OMELETS

No cookbook would be complete without a section on omelets. And there is probably no other egg dish so commonly served and at the same time, mistreated. With the exception of two restaurants in San Francisco, I have yet to see what I would consider a good omelet. The variety most commonly encountered is the plain omelet, sometimes filled with ham, jelly, cheese, or a combination of green pepper, tomato, onion, and celery. The latter often is called a Spanish omelet.

The plain omelet is little more than a variation on scrambled eggs, the main difference being that the eggs (usually three for each two servings) are beaten before being introduced to the pan, along with about a tablespoon of cream or milk per three eggs. In cooking, instead of stirring, the cooked-edge portion of the eggs are lifted with a spatula to allow the uncooked egg to flow underneath. Then, when the omelet is almost cooked, but still shiny (filling may be added at this point), the edge is loosened all the way around, and one half is folded over the other half, and is served immediately on a warmed platter.

One thing we have not discussed is how to separate an egg. This is critical in the recipe for the perfect, fluffy omelet, so let's learn how. First, this means to separate the white from the yolk. Break the shell in half, crosswise, by striking it sharply on the edge of a bowl or some other hard surface. Upend one half quickly to hold the yolk, then let the white drip off into a bowl underneath. Transfer the yolk back and forth one or two times until all the white has dripped off. Put the yolk into a separate bowl, and there you are. Should any yolk drip into the white, the easiest way to remove it is with a bit of eggshell. The yolk will adhere to the shell, but on the other hand tends to evade a spoon.

Since whites will not whip successfully if there is any yolk present, it is a good idea to separate each egg over a small empty bowl, and add each successive egg white to a larger bowl as they are separated. This eliminates losing the whole batch of eggs if you happen to "goof" on a separation.

The perfect, fluffy omelet is not the French omelette (note that the French even spell it differently). It is a very pretty substitute, though, and if done properly, sure to win you many compliments.

You will need a skillet or frying pan with a handle

that will not be damaged in the oven for this dish. Checking and seeing that you have one that meets this description, you are ready to proceed. Separate four eggs (this recipe should serve three people, but don't count on it—you'll probably have to make it twice for three or four people). Beat the whites until frothy and add two tablespoons water and one-half teaspoon salt. Beat until stiff, but not dry.

Add two tablespoons flour and a dash of pepper to the yolks, and beat until thick and lemon-colored. Then fold the yolks into the whites.

Heat one tablespoon butter in your skillet (I almost forgot, this should also be at least a ten-inch skillet), and coat bottom and sides well. When it's hot enough to make a drop of water sizzle, pour in your omelet mixture and level it gently with a spatula, leaving it slightly higher around the edges. Cook it gently over low heat till it's puffy and lightly browned on the bottom. This should take about five minutes. Then put it into your oven (which you, of course have preheated to 300 degrees) for about eight to ten minutes.

The omelet is done when a knife inserted in the center comes out clean. When done, loosen the omelet around all edges, and make a cut at right angles to the handle, just above the center, fold the smaller portion over the greater, and serve immediately.

Now, if you really want to make a French omelette, I suggest that you get one of the authentic French omelette pans, and either start practicing with the aid of Julia Child's book, or better still, as she recommends, get an expert to show you how.

PASTA

This may seem like an unusual place to throw in pasta, but did you know that eggs are a basic ingredient in almost all pastas? Well, they are. This being the case, and having nowhere else to put them, here is as good a place as any. What's a pasta?

Well! Pasta is: spaghetti, vermicelli, macaroni, lasagna, fettuccini, rigatoni, mostaccioli, linguine, gnocchi, and a host of others.

The basic thing to know about pasta is how to and how not to cook it. For noodles or spaghetti, for instance, allow about six quarts of water per pound of pasta. Bring the water to a full, rolling boil, then add a tablespoon of salt and a few drops of cooking or olive oil. This last is to prevent the pasta from sticking together in a tight wad.

When the water comes again to a full boil, it's time to add the pasta. Spaghetti should be preserved, to be traditional, in the long strands in which it is made. To accomplish this, put one end in and it can be coiled around the pan as the hot water softens it. Stir to make sure that the strands are not sticking together, and let it boil away for five to seven minutes, then test. That is, take a strand out of the water and bite it. It should be firm, but have no rings of uncooked starch on the inside.

I don't expect you to have a spaghetti lifter, so pour the pasta into a colander and drain as soon as it is done, and please don't rinse it. I know, somebody is going to say, "but you're supposed to wash the starch off." Not necessarily so. Anyhow, rinsing it only tends to toughen pasta, and make it necessary to reheat it—which is ruinous.

Pasta itself makes a beautiful substitute for the starchy dish of the meal, and when cooked as above (*al dente* is the Italian), is excellent topped with butter and grated Parmesan or Romano cheese. If you really want to go whole hog, grate your own cheese rather than buy the handy little cardboard containers that have the pre-grated. This manner of serving is called *à la bianca.*

I've seldom been one to hold a grudge against anything which saves time in the kitchen. I simply adore maid service and electric dishwashers. I also like all those little packaged mixes for sauces, gravies, etc. And if you want your spaghetti with any of these sauces, I suggest that you investigate the various ones available in your section of the country, and experiment until you find the one that's right for you.

And don't forget all those lovely package mixes. No, I don't mean macaroni and cheese, so stop sneering. It's good occasionally, but I really dig Noodles Romanoff or Almondine. Or, even those combinations of rice and noodles that another company has come out with. Try 'em. Lots of them are good, and the preparation is simple and printed right on the box. Always check this, though. I remember I finally gave away a can of goose-berrries because I couldn't find a recipe for gooseberry pie, and there was none printed on the label of the can.

I've learned since, however.

How did we get on the subject of gooseberries?

RICE

Although not pasta, I'd like to mention rice here. I believe the best rice nowadays comes in those little cardboard boxes, although you can still buy it in cellophane bags, or some places even in bulk. The nice thing about the boxes is that the directions, again, are right there for you to follow. I would not recommend, definitely not, that you purchase the minute or instant varieties. There are too many recipes which call for uncooked rice to be added, and the minute rice added to these could cause problems.

The main reason I want to mention rice here though is that, like pasta, it affords a pleasant change for the starch course of the meal, and can be used as the base for many a meat dish that is served in a sauce or gravy which is supposed to be served on a nest of some sort. And speaking of sauces, let's get on to our next subject and chapter.

CHAPTER NINE
Pouring It On (Sauces of All Sorts)

We can assume that the art of cooking started sometime after the advent of fire. (Don't comment—they could have boiled things in hot springs prior to that.) Perhaps by one of our butch cave man ancestors dropping his piece of meat into the fire. (I'll bet that smarted!) Eventually, after somebody had figured out how to work with clay, pots were invented. One of the little cave apes probably left the drinking water too close to the fire.

Mama cave woman was so surprised that she dropped a whole armload of roots and tubers into the pot, and a whole new method of cooking was discovered. Papa cave man must have come by just then and dropped his piece of meat in the pot (that thing gets into everything), and then there was soup.

Well, mama couldn't wait to tell the neighbors, and soon there was a regular conclave of three of them stirring the pot. They made it sort of a community affair, just the three of them, trying out different ingredients to serve to their omnivorous (that means they'll eat anything, honey) little families. You know, the typical things like eye of newt and toe of frog. Well, as we know, this sort of thing really caught on. We find references to it throughout history, and even vestiges of it around today. It's rather difficult to say where soupery stopped and sorcery started. (Pardon the pun, but here's another.) It's even more difficult to determine where sorcery leaves off and saucery begins.

Sauces (and their kissable cousins, gravies) are probably the most delightful thing that ever invaded the realm of the culinary arts. And making a good sauce is not really a difficult project. If you have a good taster, you have the basic talent right there. A little know-how about how to mix certain ingredients, some of them being a trifle obstinate about whether or not they're going to combine, and you have it made.

Nowadays we even have the adventures of the small, instant variety do-it-yourself witch kits (I know I can spell better than that, Louise; but, really), and I don't hesitate to make use of them when I'm pressed for time, or ingredients. I've found also that many of the condensed soups make excellent sauces, either by themselves or with the addition of a very few simple ingredients. These, of course, have been around for years, but the practice of using them as pour-ons, although not new, has grown considerably in the last few years.

There are some of these short-cut methods that I prefer to the more time consuming methods of "cooking from scratch." Some persons might object on the grounds that things taste better when they're homemade. Generally, I find this true, but I will take exception in the cases involving the condensed soups; at least in many cases. For the most part these soups have already had their flavors blended, and I'm sure that they've had to pass many a taste panel before the manufacturers would even consider putting them on the market. After all, they're in the business to sell soup, and no matter how clever your advertising, if it doesn't taste good, it won't sell.

We should also have a better understanding of the role of sauces and gravies in cooking and serving. I mention both, because they serve a dual purpose. A sauce is supposed to enhance the flavor of the dish it accompanies, and the word "enhance" is important. A good sauce will never cover up the flavor of the main dish. It knows it is a supporting actor, and in this regard—namely, flavor—it plays a second role.

However, we know that even a supporting player has a few choice lines, and this is where serving comes in. A good sauce may also well be the attractive point of the meal, the spark of color that tempts the eye to convince the tongue to taste. It's that little extra something, the added dividend. Therefore, to be completely successful, a sauce must be delicious, but never overpowering, generous in lending its delight to others, and last but not least, attractive.

GRAVY

There is probably no better place to get into our discussion than now, so let's start with a basic brown sauce. That's gravy (and groovy, too).

This is a really simple method, and I feel sometimes even more satisfactory than using what Paulette's mother calls pot liquor. Melt two tablespoons butter in a saucepan and let it sizzle just until it turns brown, then stir in two tablespoons flour. When smooth, add slowly while constantly stirring one cup beef (or chicken) bouillon. I find the canned variety best, but it's easier to mix up the smaller amount using the cubes. At this point, though, you might want to vary it a little bit and use the condensed onion soup instead.

Anyhow, any soup you choose, blend it in well (at this point you may prefer to remove the saucepan temporarily from the fire while adding the flour and the liquid—it helps prevent lumping), then continue cooking and stirring over a low heat until the sauce bubbles and thickens. If you should be so unfortunate as to develop lumps in your brown sauce, remove it from the fire and beat with a rotary beater or wire whisk.

There you have at one fell swoop recipes for beef, chicken, and onion gravies. Sometimes, though, especially with pork and with fried chicken, a milk or cream gravy is a better choice as an accompaniment to the meat and potatoes of the meal, and particularly when the potatoes are mashed.

Use only one-third of a cup of the bouillon and two-thirds cup of milk or light cream, instead of the full cup of bouillon. This is sometimes called a *Béchamel* sauce. That's pronounced Bay-shah-mell.

WHITE SAUCE

And from there it's only a tiny step to basic white sauce, sometimes called cream sauce. We start the same way as we did for the brown sauce, but we do not brown, we only melt the butter, two tablespoons of it, as in the brown sauce, then we stir in two tablespoons of flour. Again, this operation is better performed off the fire. The purpose is dual this time though: one, to prevent lumps, and two, more importantly, to keep the color light. Then add slowly and stirring constantly one cup milk or light cream and return to low heat. Continue heating and stirring until the potion bubbles and thickens.

You know what I forgot? I blush to think of it. All these simply marvy sauce recipes. I left out the salt and pepper! To taste, of course; and if you want to be real fussy about color, use white pepper.

MORNAY SAUCE

Now let's proceed. Mornay sauce. That's one you'll run up against constantly, but more likely in the turned around French fashion *sauce mornay.* Start out like you were making the Béchamel sauce, and when you start your final cooking and stirring, add one-fourth cup each grated Swiss cheese and grated Parmesan cheese, blending them in well. You might even want to add a pinch of nutmeg and maybe even a pinch of cayenne pepper to this sauce at this time. Then proceed as with the Béchamel, cooking and stirring until bubbles form and the sauce thickens.

MADEIRA SAUCE

Sauce Madeira, a basic wine sauce, goes well with meat and fowl. The simplest method is to prepare as you would the basic brown sauce, with this difference: use only three-fourths cup of bouillon (beef this time, definitely) and one-fourth cup Madeira wine. If you just wanted a wine-flavored sauce, you might use sherry, but for your own sake, use only sherry that you would drink. Never use that gosh-awful stuff they call cooking sherry. It's bad enough by itself, and lord knows what it might do to your gravies, let alone your guests. My own thoughts are that they'd never come back, and probably imply that the name Borgia is somewhere in your ancestral line.

HOLLANDAISE SAUCE

About here is where I usually pull my favorite act of cheating. Hollandaise sauce is an excellent choice with both fish and many vegetables. Its primary ingredients are butter, egg yolks, and lemon juice. Mayonnaise's ingredients are oil and egg yolks. Most commercial mayonnaises are flavored by the manufacturer to some extent, some more than others. So, when I have a recipe that calls for Hollandaise, I get out my little saucepan and put about a cup of mayonnaise into it, and over *very* low heat, stir in one tablespoon of lemon juice. Remove from the heat as soon as blended. We only want to warm the sauce, not make it hot.

I might mention that I frequently cheat on the lemon juice too. I find it much more convenient to keep a bottle of lemon juice on hand, the reconstituted kind, rather than squeeze a lemon every time a recipe calls for it. There are much nicer things to squeeze.

I'll betcha if you don't tell anybody, they won't know the difference between this and real hollandaise either. Incidentally, this is not Mock Hollandaise. That's a sauce of another color.

BÉARNAISE SAUCE

Sauce Béarnaise is a good sauce for steaks, fish, chicken, or egg—and we can base a substitute on mayonnaise. Into a small saucepan put one-half cup white wine vinegar, one teaspoon tarragon, two teaspoons chopped green onion, and two teaspoons chopped parsley. Simmer until liquid is reduced to half or less. Remove from heat and add one cup mayonnaise, and blend in well. If sauce seems too thin, more mayonnaise may be added. Then take your pencil and make a mental note to simmer the vinegar a little more next time.

TARTAR SAUCE

For a simple tartar sauce (so good with fish), mix one cup of mayonnaise with one teaspoon grated onion, one tablespoon chopped dill pickle, one teaspoon minced parsley, one teaspoon chopped pimento, and one chopped hard-cooked egg.

Add about half a teaspoon of anchovy paste to the above, and you have a *Sauce Rémoulade.*

Vinaigrette sauce is just a fancy name for oil and vinegar salad dressing, usually called French dressing. However, you'll find the recipe for it under Italian dressing. In order not to confuse, I have tried to keep recipes, at least ingredient-wise, named the same way as they are on the grocer's shelves and as understood by most restaurant menus.

FLAVORED BUTTERS

Although not strictly sauces, a favorite accompaniment to many dishes are flavored butters. For these we allow the desired amount of butter to come toward room temperature (it's difficult to work with when hard), then soften it with a wooden spoon, and when sufficiently softened beat it vigorously until creamy. If you use margarine, you may use one of the whipped varieties and save yourself a lot of work. About a quarter pound is the smallest amount convenient to work with. Then you add in whatever flavor you wish and blend in well.

You'll probably have the most occasion to use lemon

butter (made with lemon juice) or garlic butter (garlic powder is easier to work with than minced garlic for this purpose). The amount is—you guessed it—to taste. Other flavorings you might try are: parsley, tarragon, prepared mustard.

You might try one of the following shortcut sauces on your spaghetti.

CLAM SAUCE

For clam sauce with oysters, cook one clove minced garlic, one-half cup chopped onion, and one-fourth cup chopped parsley in two tablespoons cooking oil. Add one can frozen condensed oyster stew and one seven-and-one-half ounce can of drained, minced clams, and two teaspoons lemon juice. Heat until soup is thawed, and stir occasionally until it starts to simmer. This is a thin sauce and will have to be ladled over the spaghetti.

TOMATO SAUCE

For quick tomato sauce, lightly brown one-half pound ground beef and one-half cup chopped onion in a tablespoon of butter. Add one teaspoon oregano, one large clove minced garlic, one can condensed tomato soup, and one-half cup red wine (Burgundy would be good). Cover and cook over low heat for thirty minutes, stirring frequently. Serve over spaghetti.

An added thought for those who might not like oysters, but do like clams—substitute a can of cream of mushroom soup for the frozen oyster stew in the clam sauce with the oysters recipe above.

COCKTAIL SAUCE

Here's a recipe that'll make about half a cup of cocktail sauce to dip your shrimp or oysters into. Simply mix six tablespoons chili sauce (that's one sauce you'll have to buy), two tablespoons lemon juice, one and one-half tablespoons horseradish, one teaspoon Worcestershire sauce, one-fourth teaspoon grated onion, two drops Tabasco sauce (a little more if you're daring; and I am), and salt to taste. A little red wine won't hurt either.

MINT SAUCE

This next recipe makes a marvelous mint sauce, an excellent go-along with lamb or sometimes veal. Combine one-half cup vinegar with one-third cup chopped mint leaves and two tablespoons sugar. Heat and stir until sugar is dissolved and vinegar is hot.

CRANBERRY SAUCE

Would you like to get away from canned cranberry jelly? Maybe even make your own cranberry sauce? Combine two cups of water with two cups of sugar. Heat to a boil and boil for five minutes. Add one pound (four cups) of fresh cranberries, and cook until the skins pop (about five minutes), then cool it.

BARBEQUE SAUCE

And last, but certainly not least, a recipe for that all important out-of-doors sauce for the barbeque.

Into your sauce pan put one can tomato soup, two to four tablespoons sweet pickle relish, one-fourth cup onion, one tablespoon brown sugar, one table-spoon vinegar, and one tablespoon Worcestershire sauce. Combine well, cover, and simmer until onion is cooked and all flavors are blended. This should give you about one and one-half cups of sauce. If you want added tang, you might try adding a little garlic powder and/or a few drops of Tabasco sauce.

I've tried in this chapter to include all the possible sauces that you might need to prepare any dish in this book, and I hope that you will find it helpful that they've all been gathered together in one place rather than scattered throughout the book. I thought it might prove more helpful to have them this way, and sincerely trust that you'll be making constant reference to this chapter to find that special sauce for the vegetable you're servicing, or a basic sauce on which you might choose to improvise.

And if you should question the authenticity of any of these recipes, be my guest. I prefer the easy way out—but I don't always use it. Then too, think how your cooking will improve as you graduate to the more difficult type of recipe.

CHAPTER TEN

The Quiet Corner (Vegetables)

Rich titled this chapter—he may very seldom notice the vegetable courses, and even less seldom talk about or mention them. He's too busy eating them—and he's one who knows enough not to talk when his mouth is full. Maybe he thinks that nobody talks about vegetables, but he didn't count on Lady Agatha, so here goes.

The first thing that we have to consider about vegetables is buying them. Price-wise, the first thing to remember is that the cheapest fresh vegetables are the ones that are in season, and these will generally have the best flavor too, since they don't have to travel so far to the market. But what with all the modern methods of storage, fast transportation, and supermarkets we can usually be guaranteed that the vegetables we buy are not more than a day or two old. Out here in the land of C.A.M.P., we often get vegetables that have been picked just the day before, trucked in, and distributed overnight.

Freshness, being such a great consideration in buying vegetables, also leads to this observation: don't buy in huge quantities. A full refrigerator is not a prestige symbol, and decaying vegetables are not a pretty sight if you don't get around to using them when you thought you would. So buy only enough for two or three days at a time, and in the case of the more delicate ones, not more than two days before you plan to use them. True, the Furies—Patty, Verna, and Maude—tell me, "Well, you can always soak them in icy water if they get a little old and restore some of their crispness." But not even they, with all of their spells and incantations, can bring back all of the original flavor that dear old soul Mother Nature put in them.

There you are in the middle of all those fruits and vegetables, not being able to decide which ones to buy. Honey, it's almost as simple as cruising the neighborhood bar. If it's not pretty, don't give it a second thought. Does it look fresh? Is the color nice? Does it look crisp and clean? (That last doesn't apply to potatoes, which of course grow below the ground, but you can always give them a bath.)

If your answer was "yes" to all of these, it's a pretty good sign that you have a pretty good vegetable selection. Now, in addition, there are certain things, like melons, tomatoes, and other fruits that you give a second test to. Does it smell good? Just like in the bar again, isn't it? If it smells good enough to eat, it usually is. Now for the exception. When you're picking out vegetables, the bigger it is does not mean it's better. So temporarily amend your thinking when you're in the fruit and vegetable stand, and pick the smaller carrots, Brussels sprouts, strawberries, etc. You'll find that they have much, much more good flavor than the large ones. All the big ones do is spread it around a little more. Doesn't that sound familiar?

How much do we buy of each vegetable? That, of course depends upon what the vegetable is (some have more waste than others), how many people you are serving, how many courses you plan on having, and too, upon how hungry everybody is. We'll talk about general buying quantities as we come to each individual vegetable. Right now, we're much more interested in what we are going to do with the little beasties as we unload them from their brown paper bags onto our kitchen tables, counters, or whatever the set-up is in your particular little kitchen.

Whatever you do, don't just stuff all these little brown bags into your crisper and the lower regions of your ice box. Occasionally, I find that when Prissy is in a hurry that she'll do that sort of thing, and when I go out to look for something, I have to hunt through all of the bags to find the one I'm looking for, and you know that it's invariably in the last one. So, as far as the fresh, green, and perishable type vegetables are concerned, take them out of their brown bags, wash them, and either store them loose in the crisper or put them in a loosely-tied plastic bag and then put that in the crisper. The crisper? That's the little drawer in the bottom of your box, honey. If you're lucky enough to have a big box, you might even have two drawers.

Now things like potatoes and onions (the round white or red varieties, not the slim green scallions) will keep longer, so generally you can buy more of them. The main danger in overbuying and overstocking here that in a week or so they may begin to sprout—so, to inhibit this as much as possible, we won't wash our potatoes and onions until we're ready to prepare them, but will simply store them in a cool, dark, dry place. Other less perishable vegetables should simply be stored in the refrigerator.

Note on berries: don't wash until preparing to serve. Store by spreading on shallow plate, covering lightly with waxed paper, and sliding onto your refrigerator shelf.

Now that we know how to buy them and keep them—vegetables, honey, we're talking about vegetables—let's get on with how to cook them, or how not to cook them as the case may be.

Many vegetables can be served raw as a relish to be enjoyed with the main course, and we will mention this as we come to each one. But if we are going to cook them, we want to be sure to cook them enough so that they are done, but beware of overcooking. There's only one other sight as disappointing as a tired, limp, overcooked vegetable—and both are equally tasteless.

The cooking times that are listed are nothing more than basic guides, and vegetables should be tested while cooking by sticking them with a fork or toothpick. The minute that they feel tender, they are done, and should be immediately removed from the heat; and if they have been cooked in liquid, they should be immediately drained, as standing in the liquid tends to make them soggy.

There are several ways in which we can cook our vegetables, and we'll discuss the main methods right here. The first of these is boiling, and in the case of some vegetables it is better to use enough water just to cover, and in other cases the minimum-water method is better, usually not more than a one-fourth cup in the pan. In either case, we will use about a one-fourth teaspoon of salt added to the water.

Green vegetables are best when cooked in an uncovered pan, and if you happen to have a copper pan, this is even better. Both of these measures tend to conserve the green color which makes them look so appetizing.

In the case of white vegetables like cauliflower and turnips, it is better to cook them in a tightly-covered pan, as this tends to keep them from turning slightly gray or yellow. A dash of lemon juice or vinegar will also help in this regard—but please, not so much that it flavors the vegetable unless you plan on seasoning it this way.

Other methods are steaming (which requires the use of a steamer, and when we get a bit more advanced it may be well worth our while to get one of these handy gadgets), baking, frying, and broiling, which we'll discuss as we come to each vegetable under variations.

Now, a word as to seasoning. In my own opinion, I think a good vegetable needs no more than salt, pepper, and butter, but many a meal is greatly enhanced by adding a suspicion of herbs to the vegetable course, or perhaps a dash of wine or liqueur. Sometimes a delightful sauce will make our little quiet corner sing out for recognition and transform a meal into a feast. These possibilities will also be mentioned as we come to each individual vegetable.

Before we go into our garden adventure, let's take a very quick look at two items that Prissy's chattering almost made me overlook. Canned vegetables and frozen vegetables. If the vegetable you want to go with your dinner isn't in season, these are both excellent sources; and if you're not familiar with the brands, try several of the better-known ones, or ask your sisters, they'll know which ones they are; then pick one brand and stick with it, until and unless you find a better one.

The recommended method for the preparation of canned vegetables is as follows: drain the liquid from the can into your cooking pan and simmer until there is about half the original amount left. Add vegetables, salt, and pepper to taste, and then put a pat of butter on the top. Now heat, but only till the butter is melted, and serve.

In the case of frozen vegetables, complete cooking instructions are on each package, and for best results these directions should be followed. In many cases you'll find additional recipes on these packages, as well as hints on how to garnish, herb, sauce, or season.

Now, on with vegetables from "A" to "Z":

ARTICHOKES

This is sometimes and properly called the French artichoke. There is another variety called the Jerusalem artichoke, but inasmuch as it is seldom found in the market, we won't consider it at this time. When buying artichokes, you can usually count on one 'choke per person.

Now, before we start cooking them, we should wash them under running water, cut off the stem and any discolored outer leaves, and cut off about one inch of the top. That's the end away from the stem, hon. Yes, that's right, the one with all the little prickles. Now, just to be on the safe side, and get rid of any little bugs that may be hiding down inside there, we're going to let them soak for about half an hour in cold water with a little lemon added.

So far, so good. Get out your big cauldron now, one big enough to hold all your artichokes standing upright, cover with boiling salted water, (use about a teaspoon salt to a quart of water), and cook, uncovered, from thirty minutes to an hour, depending upon size. The bigger ones take longer, you know. Test them for tenderness by probing at the base with a fork.

When they are done, remove them from the water, drain by turning them upside down on paper towels or a clean dish cloth, and serve on individual plates with individual bowls of sauce. Melted butter, Hollandaise sauce, and mayonnaise are all appropriate.

It just occurred to me that there may be those among you who have never met an artichoke, and that it might be well here to put in a paragraph or two about how this vegetable is to be attacked. I can think of no more appropriate word.

Eating the artichoke is not necessarily a complicated task. I'm sure we have had much greater problems in this realm, but it does require, as do other things, a certain amount of attention. Using your fingers for the operation, pull off the leaves one at a time and dip the base end in whatever sauce is served, then nibble on this saucy, fleshy end, then discard the rest of the leaf. To a point there it sounded familiar, didn't it? Now, when we've gone through all of these outer leaves we come to a bunch of tiny, underdeveloped leaves. Pull them off and discard them. (Gin rummy, anyone?) This exposes the feathery *choke*. With a knife or spoon, scrape this off and discard. The part that is left is the heart of the artichoke—the most delicious part. Cut this in bite-sized pieces, spear each one in turn, dip it in the sauce, and eat. *Bon appétit!*

One little kitchen hint here. I wouldn't recommend putting the discarded pieces in your disposal, unless you happen to be fortunate enough to have, and money enough to afford, a cute plumber.

ASPARAGUS

One word before we go into the preparation of this little tasty gem. If your evening delights happen to be of the Athenian variety, go ahead and enjoy it to your heart's content; but, if you plan on indulging yourself or others in pleasures more of the Parisian variety, I would recommend that you not serve it. Ask your sisters, or if you happen to have an understanding medical friend, they may be able to give you a more specific reason.

Having decided in favor of asparagus, allow about three-fourths pound of the fresh vegetable per person when buying. Wash under cold running water thoroughly, and be sure to pay particular attention to the lip where tiny bits of sandy grit may be lurking. Asparagus should have the woody end removed before cooking, and this is simply done by breaking it off. The point at which it breaks readily is the point of separation between the tender part and the woody part. And when discarding this woody end, it is not advisable to put it down your disposal, since the majority of these devices find them quite indigestible.

Now, some people prefer to tie the asparagus in a bundle and cook it with the tip end out of the water in a covered pan, but, as we know, this would tend to take away some of the fresh green color. So I prefer to lay it flat in a pan large enough to accommodate the length, add salted boiling water to cover, and cook from ten to twenty minutes, without a lid—don't forget to give it the old toothpick test—until done. Serve with melted butter, Hollandaise sauce, or Parmesan cheese. Cold, cooked asparagus goes well with mayonnaise too, and is especially yummy if it's been marinated in a vinaigrette sauce for about two hours before serving. (If you take a peek back at the last chapter, that ought to refresh your memory.)

Now we come to a real gasser.

BEANS

There are so many varieties of beans, and naturally so many ways of cooking them, that it would be possible, I'm sure, to dedicate a whole book, if not a series, to this little staple. Naturally, if we want to learn more about other vegetables we'll only discuss a couple of varieties and the basic means of preparation. (Plus a few C.A.M.P, favorites.) And we'll start off by considering the green (sometimes called snap or string) bean. This also comes in a yellow variety called the wax bean, which can be treated and prepared in the same ways.

One pound of green beans should serve four people, but if you use proper care in their preparation, I won't guarantee this. Cooked just right, drained well, and served piping hot, this little Cinderella of the pea patch is transformed into a delectable princess, and you may have to double your portions.

What I've mentioned about buying young, small vegetables applies especially to the buying of green beans—the older ones are usually tough, stringy, and tasteless. And if you can't find the young ones, you're better off buying the canned or frozen varieties.

Wash your beans thoroughly under running water in a colander. Snip or break off the tip ends and discard. If you've managed to get the tiny beans, you may cook them whole, but if not, cut them diagonally (this releases more flavor) into one-inch pieces and cook in boiling salted water to cover without a lid until they are just tender—beans should have a little bit of their crispness left when they arrive at the table—drain well immediately, and serve drenched with four to six table-spoons of melted butter. About ten to twelve minutes should be ample cooking time.

For added variety you might try topping your beans with crisp, crumbled bacon; slivered almonds; sautéed mushrooms; minced onions; or grated Romano or Parmesan cheese.

Cold green beans can be treated like we did the asparagus: that is, marinated in the vinaigrette sauce for a couple of hours and served with mayonnaise.

Just for a change you might try this next recipe sometime.

GREEN BEANS, ITALIAN STYLE

Get the little buggers ready the same as if you were going to boil 'em, then heat one-fourth cup olive oil in a large skillet (make sure it has a lid, honey, we're going to need it in a minute). Add one clove slivered garlic, then put your one pound green beans in the pan and spread them around evenly, and cover with about four lettuce leaves. Put a tight lid on the pan and let it steam over a low flame for about fifteen to twenty min-utes. When tender remove from flame, discard lettuce leaves, and add one-half teaspoon salt, one-third cup grated Parmesan cheese, and one-fourth cup chopped fresh parsley, then toss as you would a salad and serve with pride.

LIMA BEANS

Fresh lima beans are not always too readily available, and there are times when you will want this rather
bland vegetable as an accompaniment to a rather spicy
entrée, so if you can't find them, use canned or frozen beans. Or, if you have the time, they are available
dried, and can be prepared according to the directions
on the package. If the fresh ones are available, however, you'll find that about a pound of unshelled beans
will feed two people.

Choose pods that are young and fresh and not the
ones with the big lumps. Big lumps indicate bigger,
starchier beans—and we want the younger, smaller,
tenderer ones. Shell the beans at the last minute before
cooking—this insures freshness—by opening the pod
at the rounded end, and the beans should slip out easily.
Cook in salted water to cover, without a lid for fifteen
to twenty minutes, or until the largest bean is tender,
drain, and serve with salt, fresh ground black pepper
and melted butter.

If you would like to add a can of heated, drained,
whole kernel corn to this recipe, you will have enough
succotash to serve four persons. Add about four tablespoons of heavy cream or sour cream to make it especially yummy. (Some people would go to the trouble
to cook fresh corn, then cut it off the cob for this, but
although I fuss in the kitchen—just ask anybody—I'm
not above using a shortcut like canned corn.)

BAKED BEANS

This is an old favorite. First of all, you'll need a bean pot. No, honey, that tired old casserole won't do. It's got to be a bean pot, with a narrow opening and a lid—so the next time you're cruising the five-and-dime you might pick up one of these. A quart or a quart and one-half size should be about right.

Now, first off, we're going to take a shortcut and avoid soaking those dried Navy beans overnight. We're going to use canned beans, and the amount you use I'm going to leave up to you. The amount of baked beans that will serve any given number of people depends upon a great number of factors, and by the time you've got that bean pot, you'll have enough experience in cooking to gauge how much you're going to need to satisfy your guests. Yes, Mabel, I'm still talking about beans. Now the secret is to put everything into the pot in layers. First, we put in one-third of the beans we're going to use, a layer of thinly sliced onions; and then we'll sprinkle on one-third of a mixture of one-fourth cup brown or granulated maple sugar, one-half teaspoon dry mustard, and two tablespoons molasses, and top with a slice of bacon cut in one-inch pieces. Then again, with the beans, onions, seasonings, and bacon, and once more. Put the lid on the pot and slip it all into an oven that you have preheated to about 325 degrees. After about an hour and a half, remove the cover and check to see if the bacon looks done, and if the sauce has thickened. If not, goose the temperature up about fifty degrees more, and let it cook for another half-hour or so until the bacon is cooked through, the onions are soft, and the sauce cooked down.

If you have a local bakery that can provide you with Boston brown bread, or if you want to try your hand at making it, it will make a complete meal when served with these beans. And some stores carry it in cans.

BEETS

Choose young ones, less than two inches in diameter, and ones that are smooth and firm. Six or seven of this variety should satisfy the hunger of you and one or two friends. Agnes, back in the kitchen, we're talking about buying beets. To cook them, we cut off the stems no less than two inches from the top, and cook covered with boiling salted water for twenty or thirty minutes in a tightly-covered pan. Don't test them with your toothpick too often though—they bleed like stuck pigs, and we want to keep all the color and flavor inside. When they're done, rinse them in cold water, and when they're cool enough to handle, slip off the skins, remove the stems, and slice. If they're small enough, you may prefer to leave them whole. Now, put them back into a pan, add about three tablespoons of butter, and reheat and serve.

HARVARD BEETS

Prepare beets as above, and slice or cube. In your saucepan melt two tablespoons butter, then blend in one tablespoon cornstarch, one tablespoon sugar, and one-fourth teaspoon salt. Add one-half cup vinegar, slowly, stirring constantly, and continue to cook until sauce is thick, then add your beets and heat thoroughly.

And incidentally, Grace, if you have leftover cold boiled beets, this is another vegetable that you can treat with the vinaigrette sauce, the same way you did the asparagus.

BROCCOLI

Two pounds is usually enough to serve four people. One additional rule in buying is watch for the little buds that are opening into yellow flowers, and if they are, don't buy. You want the young, all-green vegetable. Cut off and discard the tough end of the stalk and any wilted leaves, then cook without a lid for fifteen to twenty minutes in boiling salted water to cover. When tender, remove from heat, drain, and serve with lemon butter, Hollandaise sauce, or Parmesan cheese. This is also excellent cold, marinated in vinaigrette sauce and served with mayonnaise.

BRUSSELS SPROUTS

Unfortunately, sometimes buying Brussels sprouts is like buying a pig-in-a-poke. They usually come now in those little one-pound or one-quart strawberry boxes, covered with cellophane held in place with a rubber band, so we have to base our selection on what we can see of the top layer and trust to the integrity of the grocer. So pick out what looks firm and fresh, and hope and trust that what's underneath will bear out your judgment.

In preparing, trim off the stems close to the sprout, and cut off any discolored leaves. Then soak in salted, cold water for about twenty minutes. Drain, and cook in boiling salted water to cover for about fifteen minutes. Test with a toothpick or fork for doneness, and when tender, remove from heat, drain, and serve with salt, pepper, and melted butter. You might put a cruet of vinegar or lemon juice on the table too, since some people like to add a dash of one or the other of these to this vegetable.

You might also try serving this with a white sauce or even Hollandaise sauce, too. Go ahead, be inventive—HAVE FUN!

CABBAGE

Wash and prepare a two-to-three-pound head of cabbage by shredding it as you would for coleslaw (see chapter on salads). Then soak for twenty to thirty minutes in salted cold water. To a saucepan add and bring to a boil enough water to cover the cabbage, and add a teaspoon of salt. Drain the cold water off the cabbage, and plunge it into the boiling water and cover tightly. Turn once or twice during cooking to be sure all the cabbage is done. Entire cooking time should be from four to eight minutes. Drain, season with salt, pepper, and butter, and serve. If you use red cabbage with this recipe, add a tablespoon of lemon juice or vinegar to hold the color.

It's my own feeling that cabbage is a very neglected vegetable, and a great deal of its unpopularity stems from the experience that most of us have had in encountering it as a soggy, wilted, tasteless, grayish, and smelly lump. First of all, cabbage is probably one of the most versatile of vegetables outside of the potato. It is the basis of all coleslaws, is delicious raw, and has numerous disguises and combinations like sauerkraut and with corned beef. We'll only go into basics here, and the braver of you can experiment on your own.

Quickly, I'd like to mention that instead of shredding the cabbage as we did in our first recipe, we can simply quarter the head and cook it the same way. It does take bit longer to cook, though: usually about eight to fifteen minutes, depending on the size of the head.

And then there's one other method you should know, about, because it's particularly good to use with red cabbage.

BRAISED CABBAGE

Clean and shred your head of cabbage as you did for the recipe for shredded cabbage, and soak in salted cold water twenty to thirty minutes. Melt three to four tablespoons butter in a large skillet, drain the cabbage, add it to the butter, and sauté. Turn it frequently with a spatula till it is evenly browned (about two or three minutes), add one cup hot bouillon, cover tightly, and simmer until done (about five minutes). How's that for something a little different?

I've seen enough recipes for cabbage to fill a book, so after you use these, and want more, I suggest you do some exploring.

CARROTS

Personally, I prefer to wash them well, wiggle my nose, and eat them raw. As everyone knows, this vegetable does enjoy a certain reputation—I mean, it helps you see better in the dark, and there's been many a morning I've wished I'd taken an extra helping the night before.

Now, when you're out at your market picking out carrots, be sure to get the plump, tiny, baby ones if possible. The larger older ones tend to be woody, and although they are all right for flavoring stews and soup, they should never grace the dinner plate as a separate course. A bunch usually contains about one and a half pounds (not including the weight of the tops) of carrots, and this should serve about three or four people.

Scrub your carrots lightly with a vegetable brush. Never scrape or peel them—most of your vitamins and flavor are in the layer just under the outside, and this just wastes all your efforts. Remove the tops and cook in boiling salted water to cover with a tightly fitting lid. After about fifteen minutes, test for doneness. When tender, remove from heat, drain, and serve with salt, pepper, and butter.

For the sake of variety, you might try adding chopped chives, chopped parsley, or chopped green onion to the melted butter, or even a tablespoon of lemon juice.

For special occasions try this: after you've cooked and drained your carrots, melt two tablespoons butter in a skillet and add two tablespoons honey, one table-spoon chopped parsley, your cooked carrots, and salt to taste. Simmer over very low heat only until all the ingredients are well blended, add a dash of lemon juice, and serve. Now, some people will take great pride in combining carrots with other vegetables, such as carrots with peas. I'll admit it looks very pretty, the orange against the green and all that, but if I'm to have these two vegetables as accompaniments to the same meal, I'll have carrots AND peas, and not carrots WITH peas, thank you.

CAULIFLOWER

This is another vegetable which I consider to be very delicious when served raw. After washing the head and soaking it for half an hour in salted cold wa-ter, cut off the flowers as close to the center of the head as possible, and serve in a relish dish.

When you're picking out cauliflower, to serve always pick out the whitest head, with firm, tightly-packed buds, and avoid any heads that have brown spots or any discoloring.

To prepare for cooking, cut off the stem, wash and soak as above, and cook tightly-covered in salted water to cover either whole or separated into flowers. If cooked whole, your time should be about twenty to twenty-five minutes, and if separated from ten to fifteen minutes. You can usually figure on one-half pound of cauliflower per serving.

Cauliflower lends itself beautifully to a number of different treatments in the seasoning department. You might try almonds slivered and browned in butter, crumpled crisp bacon, Hollandaise sauce, or for something different, put your cooked, drained head of cauliflower in a casserole, dot with butter, and sprinkle with salt and pepper, then sprinkle liberally with Parmesan or cheddar cheese grated, and pop into a hot (450-degree) oven just until the cheese is melted. It not only sounds good, but looks good, and *is* good.

You have some cold cauliflower left over, dearie? Try the vinaigrette bit again.

CELERY

I like it raw, as a relish: just well-washed, separated and served, in whole stalks or cut into smaller pieces; with or without salt, cheese dip, or other condiment. I find it's good chopped and added to green salad.

BRAISED CELERY À LA HOLMES

This recipe should serve four people. Cut the root end off a one-to-one-half-pound bunch of celery, separate the stalks, and remove the leaves. Save the heart for salads—and if you're planning a soup or a stew in the next couple of days, you might save the root and leaves to flavor these. But celery doesn't keep very long, so don't just put it in your refrigerator and forget about it. Now, cut the stalks into about six- or eight-inch lengths. Melt four tablespoons butter in a large skillet, lay the celery flat in the pan, and brown (the celery, honey, the celery) lightly. Then add three-fourths cup beef bouillon, cover the pan, and simmer until the celery is just tender, and season with salt and pepper. A half cup of slivered almonds added with the celery to brown in the butter and cook in the broth gives this dish added pizazz.

CORN

One of the easiest tests to see if corn is good or not is to press one little kernel with a finger or thumbnail, and if it squirts out a milky juice and is not mealy, it is good. Most markets today sell their corn-on-the-cob already husked, and although I prefer it this way (I hate to encounter those green corn worms), some people insist that the only way to buy it is still in the husks. This is a little more work, since you have to remove all those husks and the fine young corn silk as part of your preparation. So take your choice and act accordingly. You can usually figure two ears of corn per person. After preparing your corn for the kettle, then, bring a large kettle of water (enough to cover the corn) to boiling, and do NOT add salt. Drop in your corn, and after the water returns to boiling, cook three to five minutes. Remove from water and serve right away. If you cover this dish with a napkin, it will help to conserve the heat.

There are many fine varieties of canned corn, and rather than mess around with cutting corn off the cob, which usually ends up with a lot of mushy kernels, I would prefer to use these than to try to make them myself. There is one recipe I rather like, though it's made with one of these canned varieties.

HONEYSUCKLE'S FAVORITE
SCALLOPED CORN

Preheat your oven to 350 degrees and grease a one-quart casserole. Combine one number two can cream-style corn and one-half cup milk. Add one cup cracker crumbs, three tablespoons chopped onions, three tablespoons chopped green pepper, and salt and pepper to taste. Pour into a casserole and dot with two tablespoons butter. Slip it into your oven and bake for thirty minutes. This should serve six people (but don't count on it, especially if they're the hungry type).

EGGPLANT

Now, I know that most people are just going to read that heading and skip this section entirely—so much so that I could say almost anything I wanted to here, and only a few people would ever know what happened. But really, even if you don't care at all for this vegetable, arranged on a bed of lettuce leaves it becomes most attractive when decorated all over with toothpick-speared shrimp. You can even hollow out the top and put a little sauce dish in it to hold the shrimp sauce. But enough of this. Eggplant is, if prepared properly, delicious, and there are a number of ways to prepare it.

If you'll give them all a try at one time or another, I'm sure you'll find one way that you enjoy it.

SAUTÉED EGGPLANT

Peel a one-and-one-half-pound eggplant (enough for four people), and cut into one-fourth-inch slices. Dip into flour seasoned with salt and pepper. Sauté in a skillet with a one-fourth-inch depth of hot cooking oil, until browned on both sides and cooked until tender. If you have a large number of slices to cook, keep them warm in a casserole in a very low oven.

BROILED EGGPLANT

Some people prepare this very similarly to the above recipe for sautéed eggplant. My own way, however, is to peel the eggplant (allow one for every two people, and use the smaller ones), and slice it lengthwise. Brush both sides with melted butter and salt and pepper. Place flat side down under the broiler, and broil until just browned on one side, turn, brush with more melted butter, and broil until browned on the other side and tender. This actually is my favorite way to fix eggplant (and as far as I'm concerned, the easiest).

MUSHROOMS

You people that just skipped over the last section can start reading here again—this little item is an almost universal favorite all by itself, or as a go-with for vegetables, salads, soups, meats, or about anything else. It can be served raw, broiled, sautéed, stuffed, pickled—you name it, it'll do it. And now that it's so very readily available in the fresh form almost any-where, it would seem a shame to deny ourselves the pleasure of its company on our dinner tables.

Here's one case where size makes no difference. Age does. Buy the light-colored ones, and prepare by wiping the tops off with a damp cloth. The older ones have a darker wrinkled skin and are not as tasty. If they're the only ones available, better buy the canned variety. And when you slice them, if you slice them, do it lengthwise, right through the cap stem and every-thing. If you decide just to use the caps be sure to save the stems. With any imagination you'll be able to use them the next day—on a steak, in a salad, soup or sauce, etc., chopped with melted butter on top of a vegetable—they always add a little extra something.

SAUTÉED MUSHROOMS

One pound should serve four people. Prepare as above and either slice or leave whole. Sauté in a skillet with about five tablespoons melted butter, and salt and pepper to taste. Serve on slices of buttered toast.

Now, let's try something a little bit fancy.

STUFFED MUSHROOMS

Allow about two or three mushrooms per serving, and buy the ones that are about two or three inches across, so that caps will be large enough for stuffing. Prepare as usual, remove, and save the stems. Chop the stems finely and sauté lightly in two or three tablespoons butter. Mix these with one-half cup bread crumbs, two eggs lightly beaten, one tablespoon each chopped parsley and chives (or onions), and salt and pepper to taste. Brush the caps with melted butter, and place cup-side up in a baking dish, and fill each cup with some of the stuffing. Sprinkle with Parmesan cheese, and bake in a 375-degree oven fifteen to twenty minutes until tender. Baste with additional butter during cooking to keep the mushrooms moist. Serve and wait for compliments. A little white wine in the bottom of the baking pan adds quite a bit of zest, and for variety you might try substituting crab, shrimp, or lobster chopped with the stems.

OKRA

This vegetable, I have found, is much more popular in the South, and not too often found fresh in the market. I personally favor buying this the easy way, frozen, since it has to be cooked before you can do any of the variations anyway. So, after following the directions on the package, you can serve as is with salt, pepper, and butter.

FRIED OKRA

Drain your cooked okra from above and roll in corn meal or fine cracker crumbs, and fry in deep, hot fat until brown. Drain on absorbent paper towels and serve hot.

ONIONS

Everybody uses onions, but unfortunately, very few people know their onions. They come in a variety of shapes, sizes, and color, and surprisingly enough, in spite of their pungent odor and lowly state are a member of the lily family. We have, or shall have, considered many forms of the onion in other sections of this book, and here shall only consider two forms and two recipes. The first calls for the small white onion, and appropriately enough it's called:

AUNT LILY'S CREAMED ONIONS

Cut off the two ends of each of a pound of onions (the tiny white ones with the dry skin), and peel off the outer skin. Cook in a kettle, tightly covered, with enough salted water to cover for fifteen to twenty minutes or until tender when tested with a toothpick. Drain well, and serve topped with white sauce (see chapter called "Pouring it On"). You might even try (but don't tell Aunt Lily) a little drop or two of wine (white, of course) added to the white sauce.

Now, when Dingo Stark was here visiting last summer, he couldn't get enough of this next variety— I like them myself, and if you're having hot dogs or hamburgers...what am I going on about?

FRENCH-FRIED ONION RINGS

Of course! On with the recipe. Most people use, as do I, medium-sized (two-to-two-and-one-half inches across) onions (white ones have more flavor, but yellows are cheaper). Now, here's where I differ. Most recipes say peel the onions. I say slice them first in one-fourth-inch slices, and the outer peel can be slipped simply off each slice. Then separate into rings; put in a bowl covered with milk, and let stand for thirty minutes. Now, in one bowl beat three eggs, and in another a mixture of flour (about one cup to which you have added about a teaspoon of salt and one-fourth teaspoon of pepper), and mix slightly. This should be enough to treat about six onions. Now we drain off the milk—and I can't think of a reason to save onion-flavored milk. I'm such a penny-pincher, please let me know if you discover a use for it. Then dip the rings into the eggs, then into the flour mixture, and fry in shallow hot fat until light brown, and drain on absorbent paper towels. With luck this may serve eight people, but I'd only count on six myself. My friends are always very hungry.

PEAS

Now, the jolly green whatever has a good line of these, both canned and frozen, some even already sauced to make you look like a gourmet chef by only dropping a plastic bag in a saucepan of boiling water. It's sometimes fairly difficult to find the shiny green pods in the market that will come up to the quality that he produces too. But if you're lucky enough to have some available by all means, buy them. I wouldn't recommend, however, as one person does, that you stand in the middle of the supermarket breaking open the pods and nibbling on the contents. Produce managers in general take a dim view of this type of activity in their departments.

Be that as it may, you'll find that a pound of unshelled peas will probably be adequate for two persons, and so for four people we would take two pounds of unshelled peas and shell just before cooking. Don't soak them in water, though, as it tends to drain the flavor out. Cook uncovered in not more than two cups of unsalted water, until tender when pierced with a fork. This generally will take no more than ten minutes. Drain and serve.

For variety's sake, you might try blending in cooked tiny white onions, or sautéed mushrooms, or mixed chopped chives and parsley. Serve them with white sauce—and I caught Jackie the other day adding just a dash of crème de menthe (the white variety might even go well with the white sauce). *N'est-ce pas?*

GREEN PEPPERS

Washed, sliced in one-fourth-to-one-half-inch rings, and with the inside pith and seeds removed, this makes an excellent addition to the relish dish.

Another favorite way to fix these is stuffed, and you'll undoubtedly find as many recipes for these as you have friends that cook. If you want to try something a little different, however, you might try this one:

STUFFED GREEN PEPPERS

Wash and cut the tops from, and remove the core and seeds from, as many large green (yes, Mabel, you heard me right—I said large for a change—here you can go whole hog) peppers as you anticipate having guests. Cook two to three minutes in boiling water to cover, remove, and drain. Arrange them in a buttered casserole or baking dish, in which you have poured about a cup of bouillon, and allowing about a half to three-quarters cup of stuffing per pepper, stuff each with any of the stuffings suggested under the recipe for stuffed mushrooms—plus you might even make it with leftover cooked meat. Sprinkle the tops with fine bread crumbs, a pat of butter, and a liberal amount of Parmesan cheese and bake in a 350-degree oven for about thirty minutes, basting from time to time with the pan juices. You may then serve them proudly as are, or with a barbeque or tomato sauce.

POTATOES

Although I've never seen it, I understand that one of our states has published a book which lists over 500 different ways to prepare this staple in the American diet. I'm sure that we've all encountered this most humble of tubers in innumerable varieties (boiled, baked, hash-brown, O'Brien, French-fried, scalloped, duchesse, Del Monico, chips, shoestring, etc.). Since it is the "basic black dress" of the dinner table, it is well to know a number of ways to prepare it, and we will discuss a number of them (but not the five hundred I mentioned—God, oh!) But it might be well to consider a number of the possible substitutes for the starch course of our dinner. One of the old standbys is pasta, and we have a complete chapter on that. Another is rice, long a favorite among the Southern belles. Corn, in its infinite varieties may be substituted for this course—so now we know that we are not entirely dependent for our carbohydrates on the common spud. (I like that word!)

One very nice thing about potatoes. We've all had enough experience with them to be able to tell how much we'll need to satisfy our appetites. And another, it's almost impossible to pick out a bad potato. Basically all we need to remember is that we want the larger, elongated brown ones for baking, and the smaller rounder whitish ones for boiling (or the red ones). Shop accordingly, Madge; and since potatoes do keep rather well, it's possible to keep a few of each on hand. Now, on with the basics.

BOILED POTATOES

Choose the size potatoes you want. The number you will need, of course, is according to the number of guests and their perspective (and sometimes very respectable) appetites—and you are the best judge of that. Wash and scrub them well with a stiff vegetable brush. Please, at least cook them with their jackets on.

Most of the nutrient value of potatoes lies just beneath the skin, and if you insist on serving them with the jackets removed, it is much more easily done after they are cooked, and with less waste. Cook in boiling salted water to cover in a covered pan until they pass the toothpick tenderness test. Average time is twenty to twenty-five minutes, or ten to fifteen for tiny ones. I hope you've chosen potatoes of approximately the same size—otherwise they're going to be done at different times, and confusion, instead of the queen, will reign in the kitchen. When they are done, drain immediately.

If your potatoes have nice skins, they can be served as they are, with butter, salt, and pepper on the side; or gravy, perhaps. If the skins are blemished, or it just happens to be your preference, remove the peels and serve topped with butter and salt and pepper. If you want to be a bit fancy, serve them covered with white sauce, and sprinkled with chopped parsley or chives.

MASHED POTATOES

Prepare as above for boiled potatoes, then with a potato masher (or if you're so lucky as to have one, an electric beater) scrunch them up and add about four tablespoons each of butter and milk, and continue scrunching until well-blended. If you like them creamier, add more milk and continue to blend until the desired consistency is attained. Serve with salt and pepper and gravy or butter.

There is probably no more "iffier" vegetable than

the potato, as you have probably noticed. How you will want eventually to prepare them depends entirely on your own taste, and I can only give you very basic guidelines. Experience here is one of the best teachers, and fortunately, potatoes are usually rather inexpensive and lend themselves well to experimentation. So, have a ball.

We've got a little leftover here at this point, and I think we should most definitely include this recipe.

POTATO SALAD

Actually, it's not a recipe *per se*, but instructions-for-the-basic-construction-of-a, as just reported to me by telephone from one of the girls at High CA.M.P. Since anonymity reigns there, she shall remain nameless.

Plan on serving at least six persons and allowing for this, dump into a bowl: one medium-size boiled potato, peeled and diced, per person; two hard-cooked eggs per person (reserve two eggs for garnish), finely chopped; one medium-sized bunch of celery (remove the tops and save for soups, sauces, salads. etc.), finely chopped; one medium-sized white onion per two persons, finely chopped.

Add mayonnaise sufficient to moisten thoroughly, and toss gently, adding salt and pepper to taste. Store in refrigerator until serving time. Before serving, taste again. Potatoes and eggs are thirsty critters and may have absorbed some of the moisture from the mayonnaise. If so, add more mayonnaise and toss again.

For variety and color you may wish to include two tablespoons of any or all of the following per person: chopped ripe olives, chopped sweet gherkins or pickle relish, or chopped pimento.

And those two leftover hard-cooked eggs? Slice them at the last minute and arrange them on top of the salad. Then one final note of my own. I think just a dash of paprika, just a dash and no more, adds a final note of glamorous color to all of this.

Now let's start talking about those larger, longer ones, the Idaho or baking potato, the ones that always goes so well with a basic steak dinner.

BAKED POTATO

Buy big. firm ones the ones with the dirt still clinging to them, and allow one per person, although you may want to allow one or two extra for the hungry Hannahs. Wash and scrub them thoroughly, and wrap them in aluminum foil and cook in a 350-degree oven for about an hour—or until they pass the toothpick tenderness test. Serve with sour cream or gobs of butter, chopped chives if desired, and salt and coarse ground pepper.

Right about now, I know, somebody's going to say, "But that's not the way my mother taught me." Among my own friends, there are those that have their ovens anywhere from 325 degrees to 450 degrees, and bake them with the skins buttered or plain, in foil or out of foil, from forty minutes to an hour and a half. But I do want to offer a few words in defense of the foil method. It maintains more moisture in the jacket of the potato—and there are people who enjoy eating the skins, and the lord knows a soft skin is much more easily dealt with. Secondly, a foil wrap helps maintain the heat of the potato until serving time; and, heaven forbid, if the potato should explode in the oven, the catastrophe is confined, and you won't find yourself scraping a hot oven in a desperate attempt to avoid a scorched starch-lining therein.

SWEET POTATOES

This is an easy one. Bake the same as you would the Idaho potato, but not as long, and serve with lots of butter, salt, and pepper. On the side you might put a little cinnamon, nutmeg, or cloves. These sometimes make interesting additions for sweet potatoes.

There are other methods, such as glazed sweet potatoes, and Prissy just yelled something about candied yams, but let's get basics down first, and worry about those other things later on.

SPINACH

Choose the young, fresh, crisp-looking leaves, the ones with the look of country greenness still upon them. Allow one pound per two guests. Separate all the leaves, and wash each one individually to get rid of all the sand and grit. Place all of the leaves in a colander and rinse once more, then shake gently to get rid of excess moisture, and place them in a pan with only the water clinging to the leaves. Sprinkle on a bit of salt and cook gently, very gently, uncovered, until all the leaves are wilted and tender. Season with butter, salt, and pepper, and serve with lemon slices and vinegar on the side.

This same method of cooking may be used with turnip greens, mustard greens, beet tops, and dandelion greens. And, oh yes, Aunt Nasturtia says not to forget collards. But most of these greens are tougher, so they make take longer to get tender. However, you can cook them up, set aside, and reheat when you're ready to serve.

SQUASH

I don't know whether it's the sound of the name, or whether it just looks too formidable on the produce shelf, but here's another item often overlooked. It's all rather simple, however. There are basically two kinds: summer, which includes the round white scalloped, the yellow crook-necked, and the long green zucchini; and the winter, which includes the Hubbard and the acorn. Basically, you boil the summer and bake the winter, as follows. Wash thoroughly and do not peel. Leave the scalloped variety whole, slice the crook-necked into one-and-one-half-inch slices, and the zucchini into one-fourth-inch slices. Cover the first two varieties with salted water and cook in an uncovered pan until tender. For the zucchini, use no more than one-fourth cup of salted water and cook covered until tender. Cooking time should be about ten to fifteen minutes.

And you should allow about two pounds of squash for four servings. Drain well and serve with butter, salt, and pepper.

Winter squash? Again allow about a one-half pound per serving. Cut the acorn squash in half, the Hubbard into serving-size pieces, scoop out, and discard the seeds. Arrange on a baking sheet, pulp side up, and butter liberally, leaving a good-sized piece of butter in the hollow. Season with salt and pepper, and bake in a 350-degree oven for about forty-five minutes.

Now, wasn't that easy?

TOMATOES

Buy the medium-sized or small ones, bright red, firm, and ones that smell good enough to eat. Wash them, slice them, and serve them on a bed of lettuce leaves. Enjoy!

That's the simplest way—as far as I'm concerned, the tastiest—and the way that preserves all of the natural nutrients.

STEWED TOMATOES

Allow six to eight medium-sized ones for four servings. Peel them like so: stick a fork in the bud end and plunge into boiling water for one minute, remove, and plunge immediately into cold water. Or, place all in a large bowl, pour boiling water over to cover, let sit one minute, then cold water as above. Either way, the skin should slip off very easily now. Cut them into quarters and place in a saucepan, season with salt and pepper, and add a pinch of sugar. (This is to cut the acid.) Cook gently until tender, add butter, and let it melt into the tomatoes.

Grated onion or chopped basil may be added to the tomatoes as they cook—and you may serve with croutons if you prefer your stewed tomatoes thicker. Incidentally, it's best to serve them in a little side-dish. They're a little bit on the sloppy side. Aren't most things when they're stewed?

TURNIPS

Scrub well, slice, and cut into strips and serve raw as a relish. Never heard of such a thing? Try it. It's delish.

BOILED TURNIPS

Allow one and one-half pounds small white turnips for four servings. Wash and scrub well. Cook whole with boiling salted water to cover, in a covered pan for fifteen to twenty minutes. They should be tender by then. Be sure to test. Drain thoroughly and serve with lots of butter, salt, and pepper.

This should provide you now with enough road signs to lead you through vegetableland—and just think! Now you'll have something to go with all that meat!

CHAPTER ELEVEN
Bread, Buns, and Odd Balls
(Breads and Combination Dishes)

In this day and age when we can find so many good varieties of bread on the bakery shelves of our stores, and when there are so many little neighborhood bake shops around, we don't often take time to make our own bread. It is a satisfying experience, and the aroma of fresh bread baking could prove a more effective bait for your man trap that any of the highly advertised colognes. Pick a day when you have four hours to spare, like a cleaning day or washday. The actual time involved in the preparation of bread is not great, but the rising and baking does take lime, and you can't be too far away when the necessary things have to be done.

Dissolve one package of yeast in one cup luke-warm water. Add one-and-one-half-tablespoons salt and three-and-one-half-tablespoons sugar and stir well. Measure four cups of milk into a saucepan, and drop in three tablespoons vegetable shortening, and heat to just below boiling. (Don't let it boil.) Then cool it to lukewarm. Combine the two mixtures in a large mixing bowl.

Sift ten to twelve cups of flour into the bowl a little at a time, stirring as you add with a wooden spoon. If you really want to get involved, though, you will use your immaculately clean hand for the mixing. Keep the flour to the minimum quantity possible. The dough should just stick together, and too much flour would only tend to make the bread tough.

When the stirring becomes difficult, remove the dough to a lightly floured board and knead. What's that? Well, it has to be done, so form the dough into a ball, then press down with the heels of your palms on the center of the ball. Give it a quarter turn, fold it in half toward you, and press down with the heels of your palms again. Then quarter turn, fold, and press. Continue this operation for about ten minutes or until the ball is smooth, satiny, and elastic. Flour your working surface and hands as necessary, but use as little extra flour as possible.

When through with this first kneading, form the dough into a ball, and place into a greased bowl and cover with a dishtowel. Then let it set in a warm place for about forty-five minutes while it rises. It should, during this time, double in bulk. When it has reached this size, make a fist, and poke it right in the middle.

It should give a gasp and sort of sink back into the bowl. Take it out of the bowl and put it back on the floured board again, and knead it again for about five minutes, then back to the covered bowl again for about thirty minutes.

Then back to the board again, and knead it just three or four times. Divide the dough in half and form each into an oblong loaf. Place each into a well-buttered loaf pan, and brush melted butter over the top. Then let them rise again in that warm place for about twenty-five minutes. Preheat your oven to 375 degrees, and when the loaves have risen, put them in and bake from forty-five minutes to an hour. When done, it should have a luscious-looking golden crust, and tapping the top of the loaf with your finger should result in a hollow thumping sound. This is bread. You never had it so good. Well, almost never.

CORNBREAD

One of these days you're probably going to get around to fixing something southern like ham hocks and lima beans or black-eyed peas; or perhaps you're making out with a cute little number from south of the Mason-Dixon. In either of these cases, or just because you like it, you'll want to have some cornbread.

Jackie got this recipe from Paulette, and when he served it to Dingo Stark he blew his mind. There must have been other action later too, but right now get out your cast iron skillet, put a little bacon fat or butter in the bottom of it, and put it on the stove to get hot.

Mix one cup cornmeal with one cup flour, one-fourth cup sugar, and five teaspoons baking powder. Add a cup of milk and an egg, and beat well. Put in two tablespoons melted butter or shortening, and one-half teaspoon salt, stir in well, pour the whole mixture into your heated skillet, and bake in your oven which you have preheated to 375 degrees for about twenty minutes. To test for doneness, insert a toothpick in the center, and if it comes out clean, remove from oven and turn out onto a plate, let it cool a moment or two, cut into serving pieces, and watch it disappear.

GARLIC BREAD

Want something extra special to go with spaghetti? Try garlic bread. Take a loaf of French bread or sourdough bread and make cuts, diagonally, about an inch to an inch and a half apart, almost but not quite all the way through. Spread a bit of garlic butter on each slice, and place the whole loaf on a cookie sheet.

Heat in a 325-degree oven until the butter soaks into the bread and the edges of each slice start to turn brown. *Que bella!*

ROLLS

Then for shortcuts we have all sorts of things available to us. Usually in the variety case, or some refrigerated case at the grocers, now we have all sorts of rolls available to us in little tubes. I've seen butterflake rolls, parkerhouse rolls, croissants, just to name a few. Most of these have several different methods of preparation listed on the package, and you can choose the method you like best.

One little variation that I like especially with the croissants, and it's not mentioned on the package, is to form the rolls as per the directions on the package. Then spread in a saucer a layer of poppy seeds and then place "seedy-side up" on the cookie sheet before proceeding with the baking as directed.

Another little touch that improves a lot of these refrigerated breads is to brush the tops with melted butter before baking.

The bakery shelves themselves also offer a type usually called brown-and-serve (those bakery girls are just too gay), which are partially cooked, and all you have to do is pop them in your oven for a while to finish the cooking, and serve just as if you had made them yourself.

BISCUITS

There is one more type of quick bread that every girl should know how to make though. It's ever popular and especially good with a Sunday morning brunch or breakfast. Not quite as good as a hot roll in bed with honey—but nice. Biscuits, of course, and I won't tell a soul if you decide to go out and buy one of the package mixes and cheat up a storm. I wouldn't be able to tell the difference in the finished product, and if you should have trouble using the "from scratch method," I would most heartily recommend the use of the quick mix method.

For a good basic biscuit, sift two cups sifted flour with three teaspoons baking powder and one-half teaspoon salt. Cut in three or four tablespoons vegetable shortening, until the mixture resembles coarse crumbs. (Who said, "Whadaya mean, 'cut'?" I know the glossary doesn't sound like fascinating reading, but it is there.) Now add two-thirds to three-fourths cup milk all at once, and mix with fork until, and only just until, the dough follows the fork around the bowl. Turn the mixture out onto a lightly floured board and knead, but gently, for just about a half-minute, then roll; or—if you don't have that rolling pin—pat the dough out into a layer about one-inch thick, and cut into little rounds with a biscuit cutter. Flour the cutter each time before you cut out a biscuit, and if you don't have a cutter, you can use a glass tumbler. Bake the biscuits on an ungreased cookie sheet in a 450-degree oven for twelve to fifteen minutes. This recipe should net you about sixteen medium-sized biscuits.

BUTTERMILK BISCUITS

If you would like to try buttermilk biscuits, follow the directions as above, adding one-half teaspoon baking soda to the dry ingredients, increasing the amount of the shortening to five tablespoons, and using a whole cup of buttermilk in place of the smaller portion of fresh milk used in the above recipe. Roll your dough slightly thinner, brush with butter (melted of course), and fold over before cutting out the biscuits, and bake as you would the standard biscuits. Biscuits should be served immediately upon their exit from the oven.

STEWS

Now as everybody knows, there are days when we would want to do as little cooking as possible. Perhaps we have a roomful of people we are trying to entertain, and one of them is particularly cute, and we don't want that lecherous old queen to get her hands on his (whoops!).... Or, maybe we're just tired from a long, hard day at the office, or let's face it...lazy! So, take a look in your ice box. Egad!

Leftover meat is always a source of irritation to me. I get an inferiority complex every time I unravel more than an adequate supply. But then there's the hungry type, like Miss Jackie. Lord! She can take just about anything and everything they've got. There isn't any such thing as too much or two or three inches left over. I'm convinced that's how she saps their strength and winds up winning all those butch battles. I really wish those who are abundantly endowed would get together with those less fortunate and work out an arrangement wherein everyone would be happy. But enough of this nonsense. Let's get down to the task at hand, and that is what to do with those various types of leftover meats you have stacked away in your box—oops!—refrigerator. Do you throw it out or feed it all to the dog? Now take Sophie, for instance. That dog is a canine garbage disposal, nothing less. Stews—good ones—that's where you put that leftover meat; and don't turn up your cute little noses at stews—they can be simply divine and out-of-sight if you learn how properly to make them. You can cram enough vitamins and minerals in a stew to keep him up and ready for days on end. So let's start with a simple, moderately *chic* stew that takes only minutes to prepare. And since Sophie will only get the leftovers of the leftovers, if there are any, let's call it:

STEW À LA SOPHIE

Take about a pound of COOKED leftover meats out of the refrigerator and cut into small pieces. Chop up an onion and scatter it over some butter in a skillet. Turn the gas up to low, and let the onions brown themselves (they have all the fun this time). Toss them around a bit so that they brown both tops and bottoms. Then, add the cut-up meat and let that fry until the pieces of meat get singed or slightly brown around the edges. Now add a half cup of white wine, and about a tablespoon of tomato sauce or catsup. Then some salt and pepper. Cover the whole mess and let it simmer for about thirty minutes. Meantime, boil some rice (cook according to the directions on the package), and arrange as a sort of nest on a platter. Pour the meat and its wine sauce over the bed of rice, and you're ready to serve. Pretty? Yes. And wasn't it simple?

CASSEROLES

Now just to round things out, let's try a couple of casseroles. They're good sit-back-and-take-it-easy-type dishes, and usually contain both your entrée and starchy vegetable course.

Here we have one for beef with rice and corn, one Italian style beef with lasagne noodles, and one for pork and potatoes.

BEEF CASSEROLE WITH RICE AND CORN

The first one is the simplest. In a casserole put one cup uncooked rice, one can whole kernel corn, drained, and one can of tomato sauce with which you have mixed one-half can of water. Salt and pepper to your liking, then add, on top, one-half cup chopped onion and one-half cup chopped bell pepper. Cover with one pound ground beef, and add one more can of tomato sauce which you have mixed with one-fourth can of water. Cut in half four strips of bacon and arrange on top. Cover and cook in an oven preheated to 350 degrees for one hour—then uncover and cook for half an hour more. This should serve six, possibly eight people.

ITALIAN BEEF CASSEROLE WITH LASAGNE

Now, let's try the easy Italian style one. In your skillet brown a pound of ground beef (put a little oil in the skillet first, you know how by now), along with one-third cup chopped onion, one minced clove of garlic, one-half to one teaspoon oregano, and one-half teaspoon salt. Stir to break up the meat. In the meantime, cook sufficient lasagne noodles to make two cups of cooked noodles. This should be about a half pound of the dry noodles. Cook them according to the directions for cooking spaghetti. Then after draining them, combine them in a one-and-one-half-quart casserole with the meat mixture, one can of tomato soup, and a third of a cup of water. Mix gently, then arrange one cup of shredded processed cheese around the edge of the casserole, and bake for thirty minutes in a 350-degree oven. This should serve four hungry men of any kind.

PORK CASSEROLE WITH POTATOES

Choose four meaty, lean pork chops for this next one, and brown them well in your skillet. Step two, make a blend of one can cream of mushroom soup, one-half cup sour cream and one-fourth cup water, and two tablespoons parsley, chopped. Thinly slice enough potatoes to make four cups, and in a casserole, (two-quart size) arrange a layer of potatoes, sprinkle with salt and pepper, top with a layer of sauce; then more potatoes, salt, pepper, and sauce, etc., until you've run out of everything except the chops. Then arrange them on top, cover, and bake at 375 degrees for an hour and fifteen minutes.

On those long, lazy evenings, that aren't really special events, a meal consisting only of a casserole dish and salad, and perhaps an accompaniment of French bread, may be all that is necessary. But let's look now at how many ways we might make that salad. A casserole is not a spectacular dish (that is, it's nice to eat, but it ain't necessarily pretty), and the salad has to provide the bright spot. The next chapter tells how.

CHAPTER TWELVE

An Easy Toss (Salads)

Did you ever notice, darlings, that when you go out to a restaurant for dinner, the question always is, "What do you want on your salad? Roquefort, Thousand, or French?" Never do I recall being asked, "What kind of salad would you prefer?" and seldom simply, "What type of dressing do you prefer?"

It's true, however, that salads when tossed (unlike men) are generally better when dressed. So we'll first go into a discussion of the proper way to dress them (salads, that is); and then into the various types of salads, ingredients, etc.; and then into a brief summary of the undressed, or what you might call self-made or complete salads.

Two of the most important ingredients in a good salad dressing are imagination and inspiration. (These are also important ingredients in the bedroom, and can add as much to the success of a salad as they do to that scene.) In fact, darlings, when you start getting compliments on your salads, you've arrived; but, if the way to a man's heart is through his stomach, the salad, which introduces the meal, is a major roadside.

BLUE CHEESE (OR ROQUEFORT) DRESSING

This is one of the old standbys. Rich adores it, and it certainly must do something for him from all the reports I've heard—and I haven't heard any complaints from any of the ladies in our C.A.M.P. either. This should be prepared well in advance, since it requires at least four to five hours to mellow properly after the ingredients are mixed. It's even better to prepare it the day before, so you don't have to worry about getting up in time the day after the night before to prepare it for the coming big evening. Just keep it covered in the refrigerator (but not in a metal or plastic container, honey).

Crumble a five-ounce piece of Blue (or Roquefort) Cheese with a fork; add two tablespoons wine vinegar, one tablespoon lemon juice, and one-half cup salad oil. Blend until almost smooth, then add one tablespoon sour cream and salt to taste (not too much, you can always add more, but not even Maude with her spells can get it out if you get in too much), and blend again—then set it in the refrigerator until time to serve.

There are any number of variations on this basic recipe, and you may want to try varying the amounts of the ingredients to suit your own taste, or possibly adding something like chopped parsley or chives, onion juice, Cayenne pepper, or minced garlic to help it along a little bit. But, please, dearie, don't overdo it! We're trying to help the salad—not hide the poor thing.

Before we go any further, it might be well to discuss

the various types of oils—well, at least mention them. Personally I prefer a light type of oil and refer to it only as salad oil. Some people prefer peanut oil, or safflower oil, and some of my Midwestern sisters even use corn oil. The more daring ones even use olive oil (I sometimes use this myself, but only sparingly, since in my opinion it has a rather strong, and to me not particularly appealing, taste; it *is* good for you, however—it keeps the arterial walls soft—ergo, no hardening of the arteries). But, to each his own, said the old woman as she kissed the cow, so go ahead and choose the oil that suits your own (or HIS) palate best, and have a ball or two with the rest of the dressings.

ITALIAN (OR OIL AND VINEGAR) DRESSING

This particular type of dressing is best when you have a very simple steak-and-potatoes-type meal where the salad doesn't have to stand on its own two legs, as it were, but fade along into the romantic candlelight and wine background that you have planned to lead on to greater and grander things—hopefully.

Put one-half cup salad oil and one-fourth wine vinegar into a small bottle that has a tightly fitting lid, and add one tablespoon lemon juice and salt to taste, and about a one-fourth teaspoon oregano. Screw (read on, my hearties, that's not the end of the sentence) the lid on the jar tightly, and shake like fury. The jar! Then set the jar in the refrigerator for a day, at least, so the flavors can blend—and don't forget to shake again before using.

FRENCH DRESSING

At this point I could make so many comments that it's better just to get on with the dressing—dull as that may seem.

Now, if you ask any number of your friends how they make French dressing, you'll get just that number of recipes, unless of course they've been swapping recipes before you got to them. Sometimes, as far as this dressing is concerned, it's better to just go to your local greengrocers and pick a bottle off the shelf. There are any number of good ones on the market, and in a pinch (like the times when you forget to make the dressing the day before), it's the most advisable thing to do.

Now, some people take the recipe I just gave you for Italian dressing, and substitute some dry mustard for the oregano and call that French dressing. I was raised in a different tradition, though, and prefer the tomato French dressing.

Get out that quart jar again—or if it happens still to be full of another dressing, get a new one, and start throwing in one can tomato soup, one-half cup wine vinegar, one-half cup salad oil, two tablespoons minced onion, two tablespoons sugar (if you use the extra fine granulated kind, it will work better), two teaspoons dry mustard, one teaspoon salt, and one-fourth teaspoon pepper. Batten down the hatches and shake like hell.

This dressing can be varied too by the addition of such things as crisp-cooked crumbled bacon, chopped hard-cooked eggs, chopped ripe olives, etc. Go ahead: be daring. Invent something. But, honey, taste it before you serve—I can tell you from experience what dire results can be expected from an untried recipe if it has failed, but I'd rather not.

RUSSIAN DRESSING

The Russian dressing that I prefer has as its base that old standby, mayonnaise.

Actually, mayonnaise is too often overlooked as a dressing. Perhaps because it's not considered sophisticated enough—but, Mary Dugan, let me tell you, if you ever tried making it, you'd think it was plenty sophisticated, especially if you had to rescue it from a separation mishap where you ended up with an oily, eggy mess. By all means, buy your mayonnaise at the supermarket and use it to make all sorts of delightful dressings and sauces. But I digress. Here's how to make a marvy Russian dressing, so good on chicken and seafood salads.

Mix all together: three-fourth cup mayonnaise, one-half cup chili sauce (better buy this ready-made too), one finely chopped, hard-cooked egg, one teaspoon lemon juice, one teaspoon celery seed, and salt and pepper (coarse ground or cracked if you have it) to taste. And, again don't forget to taste.

Jackie just dropped by to look over my shoulder and offered this helpful little hint. When you're tasting a salad dressing, dip a lettuce leaf into the dressing (like you would a potato chip), and taste it that way. He says it tastes considerably different on lettuce than it does on your finger or on a spoon.

THOUSAND ISLAND DRESSING

This is another one of those very popular dressings, easy to make, and like the last, it's based on mayonnaise. Mix together one cup mayonnaise, one cup chili sauce, two tablespoons sweet relish, one chopped hard-cooked egg, and one teaspoon sugar if desired. Then put it in the fridge to chill and blend the flavors. Especially yummy on hearts of lettuce, and, oh yes, a lot of people find this dressing very handy for putting in little tidbits all chopped up, like that lonely stick of celery in the crisper, that last olive in the bottle, or the leftover green pepper from the relish tray.

Now, before we get into the actual salads themselves, we have at least one more type of dressing to consider, and don't flinch.

FRUIT DRESSING

Now here's where we start getting a little bit fancy. We're going to have to use the stove on this dressing, but courage, Camille, you've got it in you, and when you're through, you'll have a real creamy dressing for all those succulent fruit salads that you'll be serving from time to time.

In the top part of a double boiler mix one-half cup sugar, one teaspoon flour, and one egg yolk, and mix well. Now put in one-fourth cup pineapple juice, one-fourth cup orange juice, and two and one-half table-spoons lemon juice, and stir well. Now! The bottom part of the double boiler should already be on the stove, with the water in it hot and waiting. Slip the top part onto it and cook the dressing until it thickens, stirring all the while. We don't want it to get too thick, just enough so it coats the spoon. Now, take out the top portion of the double boiler and set this thick stuff aside to cool off for a bit while we beat our cream. For this use one cup heavy cream, and make sure that the bowl in which you whip it, the rotary beater or whisk, and the cream itself, all are cold. Unlike other things, this stuff gets stiffest when its beaten cold with cold things. Well, anyhow, when your fruit mixture has cooled and your cream is stiff, fold them together. I know you're not used to folding something while it's stiff, but this is different. For those unfamiliar with the term, it's listed in the glossary of cooking terms.

Now that you're supplied with a basic few recipes for dressings, let's get on to the discussion of just what you're going to dress. The number of things that can go into a salad includes almost all vegetables (cooked or raw), almost all fruits and nuts, and many meats, fish and shellfish (these salads are discussed in the chapters under those headings), and a variety of cheeses—and as a result the possible combinations are infinite.

HEARTS OF LETTUCE

This is probably the most basic of salad courses, but should really only be used when you are drastically short of time, or for something quick at lunch time. It can hardly be described as adequate for a dinner salad course. But, as I said, after a hard day at the office, when you aren't trying particularly to impress anyone, or if you're cooking just for yourself (heaven forbid), it'll do. Just that and nothing more. The recipe? With a sharp knife remove the base of the lettuce, just cutting out a small cone, and quarter it by making two cuts from the base to the top. Serve with Thousand Island Dressing.

Now, on to heartier fare.

TOSSED GREEN, CHEF'S, OR MIXED SALAD

First of all, make sure your greens are (1) fresh, (2) clean, (3) crisp, and (4) cold. This has a lot to do with that appearance that is so all-important. And when you wash your greens, wash them thoroughly in cold water, shake off the excess water, then blot them dry with a clean dish towel or paper towel. What's that, love? What are greens? I'm glad you asked that question.

First of all there's lettuce—but let's vary from the old theme of the common iceberg lettuce from time to time. Experiment with some of the more interesting, and actually tastier ones, like Boston, Romaine, and leaf lettuce. There's even a red variety of this latter one which adds more color appeal to the salad. Then we can add other flavor and subtleties by including endive (some people call it chicory), watercress, and mustard leaves, fresh herbs such as chives, green onion tops, parsley, and even tender, young spinach leaves. Got the idea? The bulk of the greens will be one or more of the lettuces, and the balance is strictly up to you. In a pinch, use the packaged salad greens from the supermarket.

Now, the preparation. If you like your salads to have just a suspicion of garlic, rub your bowl (I hope it's a wooden one) with the cut side of a clove of the pungent little vegetable, then add your icy cold greens. Add just enough dressing to coat each leaf thoroughly after the salad is tossed; we don't want a puddle of dressing in the bottom of the bowl after the tossing—it tends to make the salad soggy. Yeech! And then toss it. No, not out the window. With the salad fork and spoon, silly. Work them under the salad to the bottom of the bowl and lift them both at the same time, but gently. We don't want to toss it all over the table. Keep up this scoop-under-and-lift motion until each leaf is coated evenly with the dressing, and serve immediately on chilled salad plates.

For variety's sake (whoever she is), you might from time to time add other ingredients, like sliced cooked beets, onion rings, sliced tomatoes (but make sure these are well drained), sliced avocado, celery or green pepper, or anything else that strikes your fancy—or his. One rule of thumb, however, is not to repeat in the salad anything that is going to make an appearance later in the meal. For instance, don't put tomatoes in the salad if you're going to serve a tomato sauce later on; or don't add onion rings if your main course is liver and onions. The one tends to detract from the other.

'Nough said! Now let's get on to the other or combination vegetable salads.

VEGETABLE SALADS

Almost all vegetables can be used to make salads, and the composition is entirely up to you. The following are just a few of the better-known ones to give you a start. The basic rule is to keep it simple, and try to choose combinations that look well together. Of course, use a dressing that best compliments the vegetables you're using. Now, be brave and try any or all of these combinations that might appeal to you:

Sliced cooked beets and sliced Bermuda onion with Italian dressing.

Sliced cucumbers and sliced Bermuda onion with Italian dressing.

Grated carrot and raisins with mayonnaise.

Watercress and sliced radishes with French dressing.

Cooked string beans with sliced onions with Thousand Island dressing. (Good idea for leftover beans, huh?)

Sliced tomatoes and sliced Bermuda onion with Italian dressing.

Now that you're beginning to get the idea, let's go on to some combinations that you can use with that creamy fruit dressing. Remember? The one we had to cook? Well, we might try:

Sliced red apples with halved grapes. You might even want to add sliced celery and/or chopped walnuts to this one.
Orange slices (or segments) and canned cranberries.
Orange slices with fresh mint leaves.
Orange slices with grapefruit and/or banana slices.
Pineapple chunks with grated carrot.

And then there's.... Oh! One very important thing which I almost forgot. Remember that bit about presentation? You know—making the food pretty? Well, don't just serve these salads on a bare plate. They look much better when served on a little nest of lettuce leaves.

As I started to say, and then we have those little salads like:

Pear halves (fresh or canned) topped with grated cheddar cheese and a dollop (that's as much as sticks to a teaspoon) of mayonnaise.
Sliced pineapple with cottage cheese sprinkled with paprika.
Someone just suggested. I won't say who, shredded carrots and chopped peanuts with mayonnaise. I hope they're kidding.

We could talk here about the gelatin salads, but there are so many recipes right on the boxes for these, and if you wanted more I'm sure the manufacturers would be happy to send them to you if you wrote them, that I'll consider these as hereby treated in full.

Now we'll go on to the specialty salads, which are usually served along with the main course. With few exceptions these are usually served with luncheons, rather than dinners, since it is generally conceded that those courses that accompany the entrée should be hot courses.

COLE SLAW

You may have noticed that up until now, in this entire chapter nothing has been said about cabbage. I don't know what the peculiarities are of the beast, but when you add cabbage to something (except corned-beef), it becomes *slaw*. Well, there are other exceptions like sauerkraut and borscht. And I might mention here that I've heard a delicious little rumor that raw cabbage replenishes the fluid in writing instruments (whatever that means). This recipe is supposed to serve four to six people, but that depends on how hungry HE is.

All right, let's get out that double boiler again. We're going to cook! Put some water in the bottom of it and heat it to boiling. In the top, put four tablespoons butter (all right, use margarine. I say it doesn't make that much difference), and blend in one tablespoon flour. I prefer to use a wooden spoon for this operation. It's easier to work out any lumps that may occur. Now, slowly add one-half cup water, stirring constantly. Continue cooking and stirring this little cauldron until it is well-blended and smooth.

Now, in a small bowl beat two eggs with six tablespoons sugar, one teaspoon dry mustard, and just about one teaspoon salt. Then pour the hot sauce over the egg mixture, stirring as you add it. Then pour the whole mixture back into the top of the double boiler, and continue cooking and stirring until the mixture thickens. Please don't cook it too much. Remove from fire, and add one-half cup vinegar and blend it in thoroughly, and set it aside to cool while we prepare the cabbage.

Wash, blot dry, and remove the outer leaves from a two-pound head of cabbage. Cut the head in half, and with a V-shaped cut in each half remove the core. Then placing each half in turn cut side down, make very thin slices. This in effect does a marvelous job of shredding the cabbage. Of course, if you have one of those handy little kitchen devices for such shredding, all the better, but it's not absolutely essential.

Now, let's put the shredded cabbage into a bowl, and pour the cooled dressing over it. *Voilà?* Not quite. We want to be sure that the cabbage has enough time to soak up all this flavor, and to do this it has to be completely covered by the mixture, so we put a salad plate or something on top of the cabbage to push it down into the dressing, and then weight it down and store it in the refrigerator for twenty-four hours—or more. It keeps quite well, and though the process is not as simple as phoning the corner delicatessen, the results are much more satisfying.

LADY AGATHA'S TWENTY-FOUR HOUR SALAD

This one is a favorite around C.A.M.P. headquarters. It's heavy on the calories though, so I usually reserve it for very festive occasions; and, it can be served as an accompaniment to the main course.

In a small pan, mix four slightly beaten eggs, three tablespoons lemon juice, one teaspoon salt, and a pinch of dry mustard; and cook, stirring constantly over very low heat until the mixture just starts to thicken. You could use your double boiler for this, but I find that if the heat is low enough and I watch the mixture carefully enough, I have no trouble. Then, set this mixture aside to cool while you mix, in a large bowl, one number-two and one-half can crushed pineapple, well drained, and one cup chopped nuts (walnuts preferably, or if you prefer, pecans, although these latter are very rich—just don't use that other kind). Pour the mixture from the pan over this and mix slightly. Then add thirty marshmallows, cut in eighths (if you want to use the miniature marshmallows, it takes ten of them to equal one of the large ones. It does save cutting up all those gooey things, but it amounts to a lot of counting). Again, mix well.

Then, beat well one cup heavy cream until stiff. Remember what we talked about before. Make sure the bowl, beater, and cream are all cold, and your cream beats better and gets stiffer faster. Then fold the whipped cream into the other mixture and set it in the refrigerator for twenty-four hours. This recipe should serve six people, even very hungry ones.

Well, now, that should about cover the salad line, and...what's that, Gertrude? Potato salad and macaroni salad? Well, if you'll back up one or two chapters, I think you'll find I've already covered that first one under vegetables and the other under pasta. And don't forget about those other delights, too, in their own chapters, like chicken, tuna, or salmon; and you might even find reference to some salads on the chapter on wines and liquors, and when we get around to it, I might even throw in one or two more under desserts, so patience, Prudence—we'll try to cover them all, as long as we don't get too fancy.

Here comes Jackie with another idea. I have to keep reminding him that we're putting together a cookbook—not the *C.A.M.P. Encyclopedia of Cuisine.*

CHAPTER THIRTEEN
The Finishing Touch ("Do's," "Don'ts," and Desserts)

"Do's," I think, are the most important consideration for making life easier for the cook, especially for the cook who is doubling as host.

It is generally acceptable that the hostess-cook, or the host-cook, whatever the proclivity, may leave the room from time to time to check on things in the kitchen, and even retire to the kitchen entirely in the final stages of preparation and presentation.

Herein lies the first "do." Do set the table in advance of the arrival of your guests. And, do pay particular attention to details—a little thought at the time of setting the table will prevent a lot of confusion later. Nothing is more distracting from an otherwise good meal than the host who is constantly jumping up and down, fetching things that should have been set on the table in the first place. I'm sure you know the type— "Oh, I forgot the salt and pepper," or "I'm sorry, does anyone want catsup or steak sauce? No bother, it'll only take a second." But soon you get the feeling that your host is sitting on a pogo stick rather than a chair.

Set your table, completely, then check thoroughly to make sure it is finished and requires nothing more than that the food be brought to it. Oh, and your guests, too, of course.

Basically your checklist might run something like this. Is there a clean cloth (or clean individual place mats) on the table? Is there a plate at each place (or if you're carving and serving, are there sufficient plates stacked in front of the host's chair)? What about flatware? Basic setting requires dinner fork on the left side of the plate, knife on the right side and teaspoon to the right of the knife. The cutting edge of the knife should be turned toward the plate.

Is additional flatware necessary? In the event a salad course is offered, a salad fork should be to the left of the dinner fork. Are you serving dessert and coffee? Then there should be an additional teaspoon to the right of the first one.

If you're serving a salad, too, do remember to have salad plates ready near the salad serving bowl, and make sure there are enough of them. You may elect to pass the salad, in which case it is permissible to arrange the salad plates around the table, in front of the place if the salad is an individual first course, in front of the fork if it is to be served along with the meal. Coffee cups may be set on a separate side table in readiness if coffee is to follow dinner—if you prefer coffee with dinner, set the cups and saucers to the right of the teaspoons.

Wine or water glasses, if used, should be placed at

the top of the knife.

Cream and sugar? Coffee with the meal, place them on the table; coffee after the meal, place them with the cups and saucers on a side table.

Salt and pepper? Make sure they're on the table—and even if you find that you have to use the salt in your last-moment preparations (a good reason for having two salt cellars), and have to remove it from the table, take the few extra steps to replace it as soon as you are through using it.

Other condiments like A-1 sauce, Worcestershire sauce, catsup, and mustard are of course placed on the table only when necessary. I have found it handy, and it avoids a lot of what could be embarrassment, to make a list of things that should be on the table as accompaniments to foods that I prepare as I go along, especially if I have prepared something in advance and stored it in the refrigerator. I'll never forget how mortified I was the time I fixed a Thanksgiving dinner and forgot to serve the cranberry sauce and the pumpkin pie.

Next, if possible set up your bar in the front room, on a small table or cart. All you need is your liquors and mixes, glasses, and a bucket of ice cubes. You as host, of course, will fix the first drinks, but you might ask one of your guests that you know well (maybe even him) to relieve you of this task after the first one, since you will have to be bobbing in and out from time to time. Double-check the bar, too, to make sure that everything is well in this department.

Now, to the smooth operation of the kitchen. If you

have a double sink, things will run much smoother out here. If not, I would keep my entertaining simple. The worst thing I can imagine is to wake up the morning after a little get-together and find that every pot, pan, glass, plate, knife, fork, and spoon in the apartment has been used—not to mention the fact that crusts have formed from the sauces, there are dried rings around the glasses and the cups, and worst of all, greasy encrustations on the broiler and meat pans.

Remedy? DO—do keep one sink full of hot soapy water while you are cooking, and as you have the time, rinse and wash your cooking utensils as you go along. It makes life so much simpler, believe me. And even when you get around to the serving time, you still have that sink of water there. As you turn out your foods from the cooking utensils into their serving dishes, drop the utensils into the water so they'll soak and wash up much more easily later on. There may even be room enough that you'll be able to put dishes from the various courses into this water as they are removed from the table.

DESSERTS

In these days of calories and diets, we don't think as often as we used to about desserts. A lot of my friends have started to adopt the French attitude toward it. (That doesn't mean quite what you're lecherous mind is thinking, Maudie.) They've started serving cheese with fruit. No, I mean like...sliced cheddar cheese with sliced apple, or sliced Swiss cheese with pear. It's very satisfactory as a finishing touch, and calorie-wise a lot more acceptable to those of your friends who may be on diets.

But occasions do come along that call for something more in the way of dessert—and so I want to leave you with this recipe I stole from Jackie's mother, and entered into a cooking contest that one of the local gay rags was sponsoring, and took first prize for desserts. Hang on to your gay bonnets, and don't laugh, it's good—Mayonnaise Cake!

MAYONNAISE CAKE

Mix together six tablespoons unsweetened cocoa, three teaspoons baking soda, three cups sifted flour, and one and one-half cups sugar.

In another bowl, mix together one and one-half cups mayonnaise, one and one-half cups lukewarm water, and one and one-half teaspoons vanilla extract.

Stir the dry ingredients into the liquid ones and beat until smooth and creamy.

Grease three eight-inch cake pans and pour the batter into them. I know you'll probably want to lick the bowl, or if he's there, he will, but scrape as much of the batter as you can into the pans. Then put them into your oven that you've preheated to 350 degrees for thirty-five minutes. Test for doneness by inserting a toothpick into the center. If it comes out clean with only a crumb or two clinging to it, the cake is done.

Make a butter-cream icing according to the recipe that you'll find on a package of powdered sugar (those are the packages marked, "XXXX"), and you might even try adding about three teaspoons of instant coffee to the recipe for additional flavor.

A word on removing the cake from the oven. Let the cake stand two or three minutes before turning it out of the pans, then let it cool for at least half an hour before frosting it. Then: spread a layer of frosting on one layer, then place the next layer on top, then a layer of frosting, another layer of cake, and a final layer of frosting. This is a very moist cake and keeps well for several days—so I'm told. Mine are always eaten up the first day.

Well, good luck on your cooking. And remember, if he gets into the kitchen and starts to experiment, you might have to fight to see who's going to wear the apron in the family.

ABOUT THE AUTHOR

VICTOR J. BANIS is the critically acclaimed author ("the master's touch in storytelling..."—*Publishers Weekly*) of more than 200 published books and numerous short stories in a career spanning nearly a half century. A native of Ohio and a longtime Californian, he lives and writes now in West Virginia's beautiful Blue Ridge.

You can visit him at http://www.vjbanis.com

www.ingramcontent.com/pod-product-compliance
Lightning Source LLC
Chambersburg PA
CBHW022359280326
41935CB00007B/241